Who's Going To Pay For This?

How to Keep Pension and Benefits From
Running Your Organization into the Ground

RENÉE COUTURE

Who's Going To Pay For This?

ISBN-13: 978-0-9970968-8-0
ISBN-10: 0-9970968-8-8

Published by: Celebrity Expert Author
http://celebrityexpertauthor.com

Canadian Address:
501- 1155 The High Street,
Coquitlam, BC, Canada
V3B.7W4
Phone: (604) 941-3041
Fax: (604) 944-7993

US Address:
1300 Boblett Street
Unit A-218
Blaine, WA 98230
Phone: (866) 492-6623
Fax: (250) 493-6603

To my sons,
Charles-Étienne, James and Christian,
working towards a healthier workplace for you.

Contents

INTRODUCTION

IF YOU ARE an employer, you may be wondering how you can solve the pension and benefits crisis in your organization, so that your company is profitable and sustainable, and your workforce is productive and motivated.

This book will provide some very useful information to help you address these challenges. All the material herein is derived from my 20-plus years of professional experience in the pension and benefits industry, both as an executive and a consultant.

How did I choose this particular field? I always loved mathematics; it appeals to me because it isn't subjective: There is always a right or wrong answer to any problem.

In college I decided to go into finance, but my first philosophy professor pointed out that it was such a wide field, I needed to find a niche. "Why don't you look into actuarial mathematics," he suggested, adding that he had an actuary friend who played squash every afternoon.

I wasn't into squash, but actuarial math, especially as it applied to pension programs, sparked my interest. I received my BA degree in Actuarial Science at Concordia University in Montreal, and continued my training and professional development in fields such as strategy, strategic alliance management, and human resources.

When you become an actuary, you have to pass exams from two bodies: One in Canada, which is called the Canadian Institute of Actuaries, and the other in the US, the Society of Actuaries. There are roughly eight to 10 exams, and it can take from three to five years to achieve that.

I became a fellow of the Society of Actuaries and the Canadian Institute in 2000. I started my career working as a pension consultant, really applying mathematics to a very critical part of our society.

I spent eight years at a company now called Willis Towers Watson, followed by Pratt & Whitney Canada, where I was looking after the pension, the benefits, and the compensation in the Human Resources department. It was really a great eye-opener. I was able to use my background to analyze, observe, and contribute to how the company could manage benefits or pension, and how to keep them sustainable. I also learned a lot about the inner working of a company.

In 2006, I went on to work for Canada Post, which was my second job in HR, where I felt less of a learner and more of a teacher. I looked after the Benefits and Pension policy, implementing and managing the corporation's plans, in line with the overall corporate strategy. I learned how to educate about the value of pension and benefits. I took part in negotiations with the unionized workforce, explaining the mechanics of the pension plan and why there were deficits. I also helped make benefits sustainable for the corporation.

I'm proud to say that Canada Post was one of the pioneers in managing drug costs in the industry. Now insurance companies have it as part of their designs and options; we were instrumental in creating one of the first big plans that involved managing drug costs. We were saving close to 10% of what would have been the expected cost on a yearly basis. A lot of the savings were really due to better education of the drug consumer, the employee. There often is no need to buy newer or more costly drugs when the proven affordable ones work well. The benefits industry is costly for one particular reason, and there are three parties involved: The buyer/consumer (the employee), the payer (the employer), and the one managing all this - the insurance carrier. The marketing of drugs targets the non-paying consumer; therefore, costs can escalate very easily.

After five years at Canada Post, I went on to the National Hockey League (NHL), to lead their pension administration group.

A few years later, as I had quite enjoyed working in benefits and wished to add sales to my work experience, I was privileged to be hired at my current job as a Senior Account Executive for group benefits at Great-West Life. In this position, I have the opportunity to work with employers (my clients), helping them get plans and coverage at the price they can afford. It is a great addition to my consulting experience. Then, on the other end, I see the insurer, the complexity of the insurance world, evaluating risks that are taken, and how offerings are put together for employers. In my role, I need to ensure that both parties can live in the same world and get what they need; the insurance company has to be viable and profitable, and the employer needs to be able to afford benefits.

I was prompted to write this book as I felt we are in a real predicament right now. Pension and benefits are quite expensive and instead of figuring out why this is happening, and how to best act on it, we treat the symptom as opposed to the cause. We reduce pension and benefits to eliminate the cost, while employees still need a pension to eventually be able to retire and afford benefits in case of illness.

We keep repeating the same pattern that had supposedly worked in the past, but we don't really evaluate if it produces the best results in the long run. The thinking we have been using for years now no longer works in today's environment. It's time to take a step back, look at today's reality, figure out what needs to be achieved, and start with a fully blank page to come up with solutions.

Some people may not yet realize it, but companies are facing huge challenges with their pension and benefits plan these days. My contribution to the workforce in this book is to help CEOs, CFOs, HR executives, and other decision-makers to effectively manage their employee costs beyond the payroll, so as to improve their bottom line.

This book can also be helpful to anyone who is impacted by pension and benefits – and that is practically everyone.

Before we explore this subject in depth, let's look at the current situation of the pension and benefits program, and what impact it has on your company.

The way things stand now

Why is the pension and benefits program in crisis? The main reason is that we are living too long. In many ways, this is a great thing, especially if we are healthy in body and mind. But that is not the case for everyone - another reason for the crisis is that many of us are stressed, depressed, and plagued with diseases.

Let's look at the longevity factor from a different perspective: When workplace pensions were more widely introduced in Canada in the1970s, the retirement age was 65, while the average life expectancy was only about 65 for men, and around 75 for women. This meant that the average worker didn't live too long to collect his pension. Today's life expectancy is beyond 80 years old for both men and women. Therefore, costs of pension plans went from just a few percent of the payroll to 15% plus when looking at the pension plan design that was created in the 70s.

Perhaps for some of you, your employment contract gives you a sense of security, believing that you will get your pension as it was promised.

The reality is that the contracts can't protect you. The promises made 30 or 40 years ago are no longer sustainable.

We have seen this trend in the pension industry: The benefits are also now starting to face some challenges in affordability.

On the benefits side, drug and disability costs have been dramatically escalating in the last five to 10 years. This will have a trickling effect on your business – on the viability of your company and the cost of products, of any consumption actually.

Going back to the subject of longevity: This is the first time in history we have five generations in the labor market.

There are maturists, born between 1924 and 1945; the baby boomers that followed from 1946 to 1964; Generation X up to 1980; Generation Y up to 1995; and the newest Generation Z, born after 1995, who are just starting to enter the market.

The maturists constitute only 3% of the labor force, while the bulk of it is made up of approximately 33% baby boomers, 35% Generation X, and 29% Generation Y. Currently, the millennials or Generation Z contribute minimally to these statistics.

I was born in 1972 and started with a defined benefit plan — (commonly called a DB plan) —- a pension scheme that defines the benefit you earn. For instance: "We will give you for life 60% of the salary you are earning at retirement, if you work for us 30 years." So essentially, a pension is like a reduced percentage of your salary. These plans are the original ones created in the '70s. They are costly now, adding 15% plus onto your payroll.

Many companies now offer a cheaper plan - the defined contribution plan (commonly called a DC plan). It defines what the contribution is; usually it is a percentage of your payroll: "We will give you 5% of your salary every year for you to invest towards retirement." Not surprisingly for my age group, I ended up with more of a defined contribution pension than a defined benefit pension. Younger people are getting the more affordable defined contribution pension plan – if there even is a plan.

Meanwhile, employers still have the huge burden of the expensive plans they've put in place for the older generation that is still active on the labor market or that is retired but lives a lot longer than expected originally.   As legislation protects what has been earned so far, employers can't take away what they have already given as a pension; unless, of course, they go bankrupt.

This burden is and will remain on the shoulders of the newer generations. Part of the revenue from everything they produce will have to ensure that the pension plan is still viable and has enough money in it to continue the payouts.

What about benefits other than pension? Labor market competition in this realm has been keeping the level of benefits at a more decent level. As benefits are current, employees use them now as opposed to a pension that is for the future. Still, to manage their costs, employers are transferring the cost to employees.

Back to how this is a burden for the new generation: Statistics indicate that the average age for an employee on long-term disability is north of 45. The cost of drugs peaks at around age 55. So employees who are around 55 are the more costly members of a benefits plan. Add all this up and you'll see what employers have to support while producing whatever their output is. Where are they cutting costs and who is sharing this load? It has to be the newcomers.

The challenges of the 21st century

The advent of technology has played a significant role in how companies manage their workforce. Employers don't need to be as face-to-face or as paper-based, as they used to be. And because of the growing popularity of telecommuting, employees are not necessarily sitting at a desk in one location from 9 to 5. Those are key factors that you, as an employer, need to consider when you're looking at your solution for a healthier, more productive, and more profitable workplace. Embracing the realities of today is key to the solutions to the pension and benefits challenge.

Additional challenge is posed by the many generations currently in the workforce: The older workers who are not retiring are causing delays in the advancement system. The deserving younger workers don't get promoted, become frustrated, and leave. Employers are left with older workers, who are possibly not motivated to work, while the younger ones leave, seeing no incentives to remain.

Many companies still have to deal with the pension plan path that is extremely costly, more risky, and more volatile. And, as I mentioned, with life expectancy increasing, pension plans will have to pay more pensions out and, therefore, cost money for a longer time. All this impacts the bottom line and when a company's bottom line is hit, it means reduced profitability and even the potential viability of the company.

What happens when older workers have health issues? That certainly has a direct impact on the company; when you have someone on disability, their cost doesn't go away.

The company may have insurance to cover disability, but it still costs money. The carrier puts aside a reserve that covers the monthly benefits that you're paying on disability, which is usually around 60 to 70% of pay. This reserve is being accumulated with the premiums paid by the employer for the benefit, for the insurance. This is a percent of payroll also, just like the pension benefit is.

The premium is likely to be equal to the disability payment that the carrier is paying. Therefore, simple math suggests that for every person you have on disability, you still pay 60% of their salary and get no productivity for it. Furthermore, if this individual is the typical disability case - an older employee, say in his 50s – he tends to make more money than the younger one, so is costlier in hard dollars.

Then, on top of that, you potentially – even highly likely - have to replace that person in your workforce, so that's 100% salary, even if the replacement is paid less. So this individual is costing you 160% of salary, and that's just looking at disability. You're not talking about pension costs, or about any other benefits this person is using.

When your disability premiums increase - and we've seen it in the last few years when disability incidence has risen and costs have gone up easily by 15 to 30% yearly - it is a strain on the employer. It's also a strain in the workplace, because when people get sick and leave on disability, it affects morale and increases workload. Therefore, a high rate of disability creates an unhealthy environment for all concerned, and certainly affects the bottom line.

On the pension side, another reason why the defined benefit pension plans are so expensive is the disconnect between the investment return on the invested assets and the determined value of the pension promise, more commonly called the liability. The investment returns on these pensions have been abysmal for quite a while now. Over the last 10 or 15 years, the average returns have often been not more than 6% or less a year. Of course, you'll always have the top pension plans that do active management and they actually do better. But smaller, more passively managed plans will see a lot less return. We are in a low interest environment that likely won't go away, so even making a 10% return on your assets is not enough.

When we evaluate what the employer owes, the liability of the pension promise, the rate used to determine what is owed today, is lower than what the return on the asset is. Consider having to accumulate $1,000 in one year, and you have two choices of investments: One will yield you 2% and the other 10%. You'll need more money now if you invest at 2% than if you invest at 10%. In the pension realm it translates like this:

- In a year I need $1,000 to pay for someone's pension

- My assets today are worth $910 and with my expected 10% return I will have my $1,000 ($910 x 1.10 = 1,001)

- As I know I will owe $1,000 in pension in a year, what is that worth today? Pension rules require me to use a low risk interest rate like 2%. This means today I need $981 ($981 x 1.02 = $1,001)

- So when looking at the assets at $910 today versus the need for $981, there is a shortfall today and that shortfall has to be paid in, even if likely in a year I would have generated the right money.

Simply explained, that is how defined benefit pension plans (the 1970s model) are evaluated on one given day. It is causing a real cash problem for employers today; it's just not good enough to make a good return.

Results-Oriented Solutions

Are you struggling with keeping your employees happy, productive, and motivated? Are you concerned about your organization's profitability while costs are spiraling out of control? The solution is easier than you think. Sometimes costs can be reduced immediately by adjusting your pension and benefits plans to meet the current needs of your workforce.

By combining this with management strategies that address the wants and needs of all the generations, you can have a happy and healthy flow of people through the workforce and tailor your compensation/pension/benefits to keep profits growing.

To achieve these goals (as many companies have done – I'll mention some examples further on), a major shift in management may be necessary. To put you on the right path, I have devised this 5-Step Plan to a Pension and Benefits Program that Supports a Thriving Workplace:

1. Take a look at reality in your organization

2. The major shift is needed in our way of finding solutions

3. Create solutions that deliver on promises and adapt to changes

4. Create leadership and engagement based on the needs of the workforce

5. Capitalize on the strengths of happy employees from every generation to create a thriving organization

In the following chapters, I will discuss all these points and ways to achieve a positive transformation your company needs in order to run a profitable and sustainable organization.

At the end of the book, there will be a special offer for you: A great opportunity to learn how to solve the pension and benefits crisis in your organization by implementing management strategies that help with:

- Profits for the organization and the investors

- Productive happy employees who like doing their jobs

- Compensation and benefits/pension that meet the needs of all generations in the workforce

- Ability to adapt to the needs and cost of the changing times

- A management style that works to keep employees engaged, motivated and happy

- Allows you to hit your targets and keep the organization profitable without burning yourself out

- A solution that allows you to reclaim the control of the costs

In the next chapter, we will first look at the global pension picture, as pension is really where things started to get expensive and unaffordable. We then will focus on what is happening closer to home in Canada, although the methodology proposed here can be applied anywhere in the world.

CHAPTER 1:
Rating Canada's Pension Plan – The Global Perspective

BEFORE WE START examining the challenges posed by Canada's pension scheme, let's see how it compares with other countries.

To do that, I'll refer to a reliable source - Melbourne Mercer Global Pension Index, which has been produced each year since 2009 through the collaboration between Mercer, a global leader in pension funds management, and the non-profit research center, Australian Centre for Financial Studies.

As Mercer explains on its website, "The primary objective of this research is to benchmark each country's retirement income system using more than 40 indicators. An important secondary purpose is to highlight the shortcoming in each country's system and to suggest possible areas of reform that would provide more adequate retirement benefits, increased sustainability over the longer term and/or a greater trust in the pension system."

Where we stand

So how does Canada rank in the Mercer Index? It is positioned among the top 10 nations with the world's best pension systems, after Denmark, the Netherlands, Australia, Sweden, and Switzerland.

In 2015 (the last year for which statistics were available at the time of writing of this book), Canada received a score of 70 on a scale between 0 and 100, based on factors such as adequacy, integrity, and sustainability.

The top two countries (out of 25 examined) were Denmark and the Netherlands, which received a score of 81.7 and 80.5, respectively. (The USA, with a score of 56.3, was in the 14th place).

How are these factors determined, you may wonder? Here's the explanation:

Adequacy:

The primary objective of any pension system is to provide adequate retirement income. This sub-index considers the base level of income provided, as well as the net replacement rate for median-income earners.

Sustainability:

This sub-index evaluates the long-term sustainability of the current retirement income system, particularly in the light of the ageing population, the increasing ratio of retirees to productive workers and, in some countries, increasing government debt.

Integrity:

It is critical that a nation has confidence in the ability of private sector pension providers to deliver retirement benefits over many years into the future. This sub-index therefore considers the role of regulation and governance, the protection provided to participants, and the level of communication provided to members. We consider the requirements set out in relevant legislation, as well as an indicator based on the World Bank's Worldwide Governance indicators.

The top scorers, Denmark and the Netherlands rated so high, Mercer said, because they both have "a first class and robust retirement income system that delivers good benefits, is sustainable and has a high level of integrity."

Canada, on the other hand, has "a system that has a sound structure, with many good features, but has some areas for improvement."

What areas are those and how can they be improved? According to Mercer, this could be achieved by:

- Increasing the coverage of employees in occupational pension schemes through the development of an attractive product for those without an employer-sponsored scheme.

- Increasing the level of household savings.

- Increasing the labor force participation rate at older ages.

This gives you an appreciation for where Canadians stand as to pension schemes. In this book, we will not so much discuss global solutions to the pension issue, but rather what the employer's role can be with respect to pension on any given budget.

More data

If you remember in the Introduction, I described the two main types of plans — the DB plan, which is a much safer but costlier promise compared to the DC plan. A 2016 report by Willis Towers Watson found the following:

- Canada has the sixth largest share of pension assets worldwide.

- Assets under management of the world's largest pension funds totaled US$35,316 billion in 2015, a decrease of 0.9% since the end of 2014.

- Funds made a return of 5.1% on average per year in USD from 2005 to 2015. For Canada it was 5.8%.

- Over the last 10 years ending in 2015, there has been an increase in DC plan assets of 8%. This has shifted the asset split between DB plans and DC plans to 52% in DB and 48% in DC respectively.

- Interestingly, Australia leads with 87% of plans being DC plans and only 13% being DB plans, and yet had a 9.1% average annual return in USD over the last 10 years.

Not all pensions are created equal

I mentioned the ranking of the world's best pensions, but obviously not every country has an adequate pension system in place. Developing and emerging nations, for instance, are still far behind advanced countries when it comes to securing retirement income for their population.

According to Natixis Global Retirement study 2016, which is based on data from the World Bank and World Health Organization, among other sources, the bottom 10 countries (out of 43 nations surveyed) in terms of pension security are Greece, Brazil, Russia, Turkey, China, Spain, Cyprus, Mexico, Portugal, and India. (India, by the way, also rates the lowest on the Mercer Index).

The so-called "transition economies" – Eastern European countries that used to be part of the Soviet bloc – are also experiencing problems. According to a recent World Bank report, many are faced with having to support large numbers of the elderly through pensions financed by contributions from a markedly smaller number of workers. "As a result, regardless of whether these countries are old or young, their pension systems require significant support from the government," the report states.

It goes on to say that "some of the countries with pension systems that will be fiscally sustainable in the future have achieved that goal through considerable current or future lowering of benefit levels. At some point, these benefits may not be adequate, and social assistance may need to augment them, in addition to covering the elderly who fall outside the contributory system."

Furthermore, 77% of individual investors surveyed believe they will have to assume greater responsibility for funding their retirement.

Global challenges
(demographics + economy)

Although structural and other differences exist among various nations' pension schemes, they share many common challenges – as you can see above. The Mercer report makes it clear that "Many of the challenges relating to ageing populations are similar, irrespective of each country's social, political, historical or economic influences."

Nearly all pension systems are under a lot of pressure due to two major factors: rising life expectancies and low returns on investments.

What can be done to reverse this trend? According to Mercer, it's all about policy reforms that will encourage people to work longer, the level of funding for retirement, and "some benefit design issues that reduce leakage of benefits before retirement."

This is a brief global view of the pension schemes. It gives us a good idea of where Canada is positioned on this very wide spectrum and shows that our challenges are not that unique.

A global benefits comparison is purposely not done here as benefits delivery in the world are affected by too many variables. To name a few, the wide spectrum of public vs private split in the delivery of benefits, access to benefits, and availability of information. The review is beyond the scope of this book and would have been a book in itself. It suffices to say that in North America and more particularly in Canada, benefits are available and are part of the compensation package of many employers.

The question we are going to address in this book is two-fold: How and why did our pension and benefits problem arise and, even more importantly, how can we solve it?

In the following chapter, we will look at the Canadian pension and benefits crisis from a historic perspective, and then, in following chapters, we will explore various strategies and solutions employers can implement in their organizations.

CHAPTER 2:
The Pension and Benefits Crisis: We're Heading for the Abyss!

WHEN THE FIRST workplace pension plan was implemented in Canada in 1874, retirement, as we know it today, was not an option.

First of all, as I already mentioned in the Introduction, a lot of people did not live to the ripe old age of 65. And even if they did reach it, many continued working to support themselves and their families.

In the 1800s, Canada was still a predominantly agrarian society, so most people farmed or were traders and craftsmen. But the development of industry and expansion of railroads in the second half of the 19th century changed that.

In 1874, the Grand Trunk Railway Company created a pension plan that required the workers to join by age 37 and remain employed until at least 55. The plan deferred part of their wages until retirement, as a way to ensure the workers' loyalty. By 1900, only federal employees, railway workers, and employees of some banks were covered by pension plans.

The first Canadian legislation that encouraged workers to save for their retirement was the *Canadian Government Annuities Act* of 1908. As its name suggests, the purpose of this legislation was to encourage Canadians to prepare for their retirement by purchasing a government annuity, which would yield fixed yearly benefits at a specified age. However, few Canadians could afford to buy this plan.

In the early days, there was not much actuarial knowledge of funding pensions. Companies treated them as current expenses, and had no reserves.

A wake up call came in 1923 from the US, where a meat processing plant, the Morris Packing Company, went bankrupt and stopped all payments to its 400 retirees. Current employees who had paid into to the pension plan had lost their contributions too.

In the aftermath of this fiasco, suggestions for the reform of the system were raised, specifically that pension costs should be accrued, with funds held by an independent fiduciary.

Many corporations, however, resisted these reforms for purely self-serving reasons. Actuarial costs were difficult to estimate because benefits were based on final salaries; besides, employers didn't want another institution to administer pensions because they could better use the funds themselves. And this would also allow them to manage their workforce by giving pensions to reward only long-serving employees.

This mindset started to change in both the US and Canada after WWII, with the growth of trade unions and collective bargaining. Unions began to push for industry-wide standards for pensions.

In 1951, the government passed the *Old Age Security Act* - a federally funded pension for people 70 years and over, except Status Indians. The maximum Old Age Security pension was $40 per month or $480 per year.

Another milestone came in 1966, when a compulsory scheme for salaried and self-employed workers between the ages of 18 and 70, called Canada Pension Plan (CPP), came into existence. A similar program, the Quebec Pension Plan, was enacted the same year.

At the origin of the latter plan was the Quebec government's desire to retain control of pension fund reserves for investment in provincial development. The other provinces also had the option of establishing their own plans, but none did.

Over the next five years, the eligible age for both the Old Age Security pension and the Canada Pension Plan would be set at 65.

A different reality

So many executives are asking: "Why are pensions costing so much?" and "How did we get here?"

That's why the historical perspective is important - it shows how both the workforce and the pensions evolved over the years and what protective measures were put into place.

Unemployment insurance and worker's compensation also made their appearance. Additionally, employers started to provide health insurance for drugs, life insurance, as well as short and long-term disability insurance. That's certainly a long way since the first, modest pensions of the 19th century.

Initially, we needed our employees to go to work and we needed them to be able to work, so it made sense to pay them some money to keep them healthy enough to produce.

During the Industrial Era, a career generally lasted a lifetime, but life expectancy was a lot lower.

As I mentioned earlier, just a generation ago, people lived, on average, into their 60s, so if they worked until 65 but died soon after, there wasn't much payout in terms of pension. Under these circumstances, a pension was affordable. The employers thought they'd be paying out for just a few years. Today, many people live, and receive pensions, past their 80s, and likely retired earlier than age 65. So the answer to the question, "Why are pensions costing so much?" is pretty clear.

So decades ago, benefits were affordable. Initially, the majority of plans were 2% for every year of work - the maximum that Revenue Canada currently still allows. If you worked 30 years, at retirement you would get 60% of your salary. Remember that life expectancy was not an issue at the time, meaning that most people didn't collect their pensions for as long as they do now. So, all in all, employers could afford those pension schemes.

Obviously, there were no sophisticated computers to predict scenarios and create forecasts for the future. Employers didn't think, "Well, how much is this going to cost in 10 years?" It was more of a short-term vision because nobody could foresee that people would be living longer and working longer.

In the late '90s and early 2000s we began to see the signs that CPP might not be around in the future. That was when things started to change. With the financial crisis of 2008, for instance, many pension plans suffered investment losses and went deeply into deficit. That year, according to 2008 figures from Statistics Canada, only 38% of paid workers had a company- sponsored pension plan as part of their compensation. By 2014, the statistics was 38.1%.

The figure has therefore not changed much. Of the 38.1%, 51.3% of the employees with pensions plans are in the public sector, which leaves only 18.5% of the pension plans in the private sector. Yet the population is aging, looking to retire, creating the pressures we talked about already, slowing down promotions and adding to costs in benefits.

And there have been other changes along the way as well. When the pensions first came into existence (and for a long time afterwards) medications were in their infancy. Aspirin, for instance, was only developed in 1897, and the first antibiotic, the penicillin, was produced in 1928.

True, people didn't live as long back then, but they also weren't as sick. Or, rather, they didn't take as many "sick days" off as they do today, or pop as many pills because, as I just mentioned, the pharmaceutical industry was not yet developed.

Also, there was a different work ethic – it was unthinkable to call in sick because of pulling a muscle in the back, a headache, a stomachache, or for being "under the weather." They just wouldn't miss a day's work – it was unthinkable. It is not so today - a study released by the Conference Board of Canada in 2013 shows that an average worker misses 9.3 days of work per year; this absenteeism costs the economy $16.6 billion annually! Interestingly, the report indicates that Canada's absenteeism rate is higher than in the United States or the United Kingdom.

Rising costs

It is not difficult to figure out what the root of the problem is: We have a system that was designed for the time that is long gone, yet we are still expecting the same promises to be kept despite the changing demographics and financial realities. What happened when we set up this pension and benefits system is that we created expectations that are no longer realistic, for all the reasons outlined above.

The same can be said about health insurance. In the beginning it was intended for employees only. But then they started asking, "What if my wife gets sick? And what about my children?" So coverage was expanded to spouses and children, and accidental death insurance was added on too.

As you can see, a scheme that started out small and affordable, gradually morphed into a big and costly program that is not sustainable in the long run. As a result, employers wanted their workers to share the costs of their pensions. Many companies now offer benefits with a cost sharing with the employees, or do not provide the benefits altogether. Some companies do not provide long-term disability, as it is considered too costly.

Benefits are a percentage of the payroll. Life insurance and disability are tied to how much a worker is paid. Benefits like medications are not, but they just get factored in as a percentage.

There is no doubt that the cost of having an employee has risen dramatically. One could argue that is the reason wage increases have diminished significantly. Since 2008, a lot of employers are giving little to no salary increase, or barely covering the cost of inflation.

There's also another factor that has affected the cost: The decreasing interest rate, which started to dive in the 90s and hasn't rebounded since then. The impact of low interest rates is simple: I used to get 10 or even 15% on my investments 20 years ago, but today, if I am lucky, I'll have 2 or 5%. And if I'm trying to put money aside to pay for something in the future, I'm going to have to save much more money now than I used to in order to achieve my goal.

DEPOSIT INTEREST RATE IN CANADA

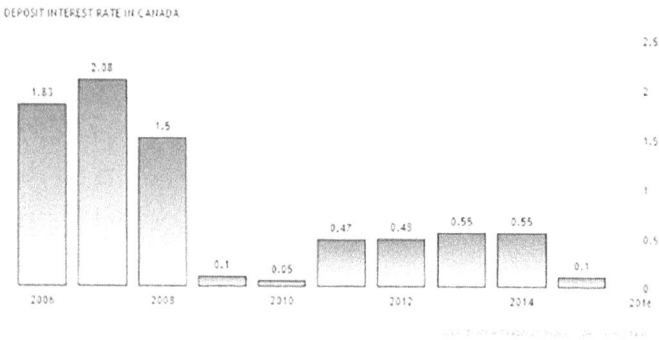

It is not surprising, then, that another Conference Board of Canada study has found that employee benefits are a significant expense for Canadian companies—in 2015, the average cost of providing benefits for a full-time employee is $8,330.

This figure does not include the cost of the pension plan.

According to an article in the Toronto Star of September 2016, "Like virtually all other private-sector workers, new hires at car factories will be given a glorified RRSP savings account. These so-called "defined contribution" plans get matching employer contributions but remain at the mercy of the stock market for decades to come, without the security of annuitized payments upon retirement.

For example, just recently (at the time this book is being written in the Fall of 2016), General Motors in Ontario agreed, after negotiations with Unifor, to move all new hires to a defined contribution pension plan, instead of a hybrid plan that included some defined benefit elements.

Since that hybrid pension plan went into effect in 2012, General Motors has not hired a single new worker in Canada. With the new pension in place, this will likely change, especially in facilities like St. Catharines, where 97% of employees are eligible for retirement."

As the article points out, this trend is not limited to the auto industry, but is more widespread: "For example, Air Canada has faced major pension liabilities in recent years, while upstart start-up airlines like Porter were free from such legacy costs and financial risks because their newly hired workers weren't getting 'defined benefit' plans backstopped by the company.

A second development last week tells the story of our pension peril from a different angle: While autoworkers were surrendering full pensions for new hires, steelworkers were fighting to rescue and reclaim their full defined benefit pensions."

That's the situation in the private sector. What about public pensions? Let's just say there's bad news and there's good news, depending on whether you have a short or long-term perspective.

In June of 2016, federal, provincial and territorial finance ministers reached an agreement to expand the Canada Pension Plan, designed to address the shortfall in middle-income retirement planning - a result of disappearing corporate pensions.

However, data released by the Finance Department shows that CPP changes will have a temporary impact on jobs — lowering current employment-growth projections by up to 0.07% between now and 2025.

As the Toronto Star notes, "The government says the pension changes will also trim the forecast for real gross domestic product growth by up to 0.05% over the short term. But beyond the year 2025, the government predicts the pension changes will result in increased GDP growth of up to 0.09% and a 0.06% increase in employment."

Points to remember:

The pension and benefits program was designed to meet the needs of workers at another time. But the requirements of today's multi-generational labor market are totally different because of mounting costs and expectations.

In the next chapter, we'll explore more in depth the different needs of each generation that is currently active in the workplace.

CHAPTER 3:

Challenges of Managing Five Generations in the Workplace

IF YOUR COMPANY employs a multi-generational workforce, managing this diverse group of individuals can be quite a challenge. You have the older employees, who for example, are used to looking up instructions in a manual, or remember details off the top of their heads, and then, you have the young ones, who rely on technology for any information and are connected to social media 24/7.

How does an employer successfully manage workers born in different eras, especially since each of these age groups has different needs and expectations, both in terms of demands they've placed on the benefits program, and what has been promised to them in terms of pension?

Let's explore this subject further.

A generation gap

For the first time in history we have five generations working side by side in the labor market.

There are maturists, born between 1924 and 1945; the baby boomers that followed from 1946 to 1964; Generation X up to 1980; Generation Y up to 1995; and the newest Generation Z, born after 1995.

The maturists constitute only 3% of the labor force. Approximately 33% are baby boomers, 35% are Generation X, 29% Generation Y, and the millennials, or Generation Z, who are just starting to enter the market.

Let's look at maturists first. They came of age during the Great Depression and World War II, so they're used to hardships. When the older maturists entered the labor market, sometime around 1942, their work environment was totally different from what it is today (it was even different from what the baby boomers experienced).

For one, employees in those days were eons away from technological advances we take for granted today. Secondly, very few women worked and men were often the sole breadwinners (though this dynamic did change somewhat during WWII, when women held jobs in such "unladylike" fields as munitions manufacturing).

This generation has what we call "defined benefits pension," and a very generous one at that. So why are they not retiring? Perhaps it's because they've seen their parents work long and hard and have developed the same kind of dedication. They also do not necessarily all have great pensions.

What about the baby boomers? They have the lion's share of the benefits in two ways. They kept their rich pensions when companies tried to reduce pensions because they were grandfathered in. Also, they're at the time of their life when they're using benefits more. Just to provide drugs and paramedical benefits, the average cost of a person in this age group is easily $2,500 to $3,000 a year. It isn't unusual for the annual drug consumption to be over 20 prescriptions a year, going as high as 40 as they get closer to retirement.

The Generation X-ers were raised during a time of changing traditional values – women were working alongside men, and not just in typically "feminine" jobs like teaching or nursing. In fact, the Equal Rights Amendment was passed in the US in1972, giving women opportunities they had never had before. The Canadian equivalent, Charter Section 28, was ratified as a section of the Canadian Constitution in 1982.

The X-ers' pension and benefits are less generous than those of the two older groups, because their employers had to control their pension-related costs.

The Generation Y-ers or "millennials" grew up in a time of fast-paced changes. Both at home and in the workplace, they rely on technology and modern communication tools like email, skyping, and texting. Often, their attitude towards their employers is not, "Oh, thank you for the job. I feel grateful," but "What can you do for me?" Unlike their fathers and grandfathers, they're not likely to stay in one job their entire lives, and are more mobile and flexible.

The "millennials'" younger counterparts, the Generation Z-ers, are growing up in a global, fast-paced and connected society, with sophisticated, ever evolving technological advances. It's too early to draw any conclusions about their performance in the workforce, but they will likely be as demanding as the Y-ers.

Shaped by different life experiences and frames of reference, their attitudes toward their jobs and intrinsic work values vary as well.

For instance, a study carried out by San Diego University a few years ago showed that the millennials are more likely than their elders to value leisure time over work. Nearly twice as many people in the Generation Y group as in the baby boomers group said that having a job with more than two weeks' paid vacation was "very important."

And nearly 75% of boomers said they expected work to be a central part of their lives, compared with only 63% of millennials, who also value workplace perks such as creativity, individualism, and flexible hours, more than older generations.

Work–life balance

As this study demonstrates, younger workers are much more interested than their older counterparts in having a rewarding work experience and balancing out their careers with leisure activities.

This is not at all surprising, given that people from the maturist and boomer generations grew up in more austere times, when work was considered to be the means of survival - feeding one's family and paying one's bills - and not expected to be a rewarding or satisfying experience.

Of course, things are different now because our lives are different.

As I mentioned, when the older generations entered the labor market, men were breadwinners and women stayed home and took care of the family. Some women did work – as secretaries, nurses, teachers, and sales ladies - but they almost always quit their jobs when they married. This was a socio-cultural rule but also a matter of logistics: Child-care centers and facilities as we know them today were not as common, so women had no choice but to stay home.

But today's dynamic is different – not so much for the maturists and boomers, but certainly for people born after 1970. In this group, you often see both spouses working, and children being cared for by a third party.

Of course, a more open attitude that makes it possible for women to join the labor force is a double-edged sword. On one hand, it enables women to earn money and achieve professional success. But on the other hand, for many women work is not a matter of choice but of necessity: They have to work to supplement their husband's income, or because they are single mothers and must support themselves and their children.

This kind of situation sometimes creates additional stress on the workforce. People might have to take more time off because they can't cope with everything that is expected of them. When that happens and workers get sick (either physically or mentally), the employer is expected to take care of their problems. And the pension and benefits programs have to provide for that. This is what I refer to as the life cycle phenomena in the workplace; depending on where you are at in your life, you will need a different job proposition from your employer.

New work models

In Canada, an employee who falls ill or suffers from work-related injury can take a sick leave or even a mental day off, if the problem is more psychological than physical.

Government statistics indicate that in 2015, Canadian workers missed, on average, 7.4 days of work due to illness. This number is highest in Quebec (9.3 days) and lowest in Alberta (5.5 days).

People will, of course, continue to get sick. And while certain illnesses can't be prevented, especially if they are contagious, the incidence of work-related mental distress can, in the very least, be reduced.

How? That would require an innovative and open-minded approach. One of the problems is the work model we've been following, the eight-hour workday, dates back to the '60s, '70s, and '80s, and is no longer relevant today.

There's still not enough acceptance in corporate culture of part-time work, or a workday with less hours, for those who want it. I know that I, for one, would welcome it because it would give me more time for my personal life and personal tasks. It would result in lower pay but a better quality of life.

In this day and age where you can literally read your emails while you're in the bathroom, why is it that companies still think that you're only productive when you're sitting at your desk?

There's a lot to be said about the advantages of a six-hour workday. The evidence comes from abroad, namely Sweden, where some companies are testing the concept of a six-hour workday at full pay. Now, some employers might argue that paying full salaries for less work is not profitable. But wait – the Swedish experiment has shown that employees get sick less often, have lower stress levels, and work harder. The result is every employer's dream: A happier and more productive workforce.

A six-hour workday would appeal to a lot of people, among them the "Sandwich" Generation, so named because they fit neatly between the boomers and the Y-ers. They are typically in their 30s and 40s, and are bringing up their own children and caring for their ageing parents at the same time. Because of all these responsibilities, they could benefit from more free time. And this isn't going away - as the X-ers get older, they will be replaced with the Y-ers, who will have similar challenges.

As seen, this concept is already happening in Sweden, and is also starting to pop up in Canada and the United States. I met a very young woman who started her own business in the IT industry in Montreal: Stephanie Liverani, co-founder of Crew Labs, and she tailors to the needs of her employees. It's a small company, but it shows that employers can be flexible and accommodating. If you trust your workers, they will not let you down; they will work harder and be productive to justify your trust.

So if you are an employer, don't shy away from adapting this particular model in your company. You'll be rewarded with more productive and healthier workers.

But what about the bottom line?

If you're an employer, you're probably a bit out of your comfort zone when you think about the impact the six-hour (or any flexible) workday could have on your finances. You worry about giving benefits to part-timers because the cost could be the same as it is for a full-time employee.

You might also be asking yourself: "Do I have the ability to adapt to the needs and costs of the changing times? Can I offer pension and benefits that meet the expectations of my multi-generational workforce? And what management style will keep employees happy, healthy, and motivated, while my organization remains profitable?"

Those are all valid and important questions. You're asking them because the new work model might be perceived as costly. But that little extra cost will give you a more engaged and invested employee. I've proved it to myself working six hours instead of seven and a half. I'm less drained and more productive.

Fact is, you can run a profitable and sustainable organization, and solve the pension and benefits crisis, by implementing management strategies that encourage personal responsibility and care for the employees. I am very fond of Starbucks' CEO Howard Schultz and his leadership style. In a letter that he sent on July 11, 2016, to all his employees (he refers to as partners), he wrote:

> "I also want to address scheduling, since I know this is an important and ongoing issue for many partners. Just as some of our customers' routines change during the summer, so too do some of yours. While we have made progress over the years in providing more stability and consistency in scheduling, our field leaders are committed to make every effort to help you meet your specific scheduling needs especially when it comes to ensuring your benefits eligibility going forward. To that end, please know that you have my personal commitment that we will work with every partner to ensure you have the hours you need."

The whole letter is worth reading. As an employee myself, I wish I had received such a letter. Mr. Schultz does challenge the institutional practices we all follow; he was one of the first to offer comprehensive health benefits for employees who work 20 hours or more a week, as opposed to providing it only to full time workers.

Think about this: You have employees who work fewer hours, but because they are less stressed and less tired, they are also healthier. And healthy workforce is a productive workforce that takes less sick or mental days off and, therefore, costs less.

On the other hand, you have employees who work eight hours a day. Admittedly, in our faster-paced reality of today, it's difficult to concentrate on work for that many hours and still stay alert. Studies show that two of the main causes of work-related accidents are fatigue and stress.

And what happens when a worker is injured or ill but your company still has to be productive?

It's simple: Other employees have to perform the extra tasks, which means they too are now overworked, stressed, and prone to accidents or illnesses. And that incurs the extra cost because the absent workers still have to be paid.

As your incidence in absenteeism due to illness rises, you will see your cost go up as well. You can easily see increases of 30% or 40% in insurance premiums.

By the way, the average age of people on disability is 45 and up for many employers– in other words, the older employees. They have higher salaries and are therefore costlier to an organization.

And if people of this age group go on disability, they'll probably stay on disability until they retire.

In addition, many people in this age group are now taking biologic medications for conditions like arthritis, and that's another cost that employers are shouldering. In my experience, a vast majority – possibly even 90% - of companies have paid for at least one claim, which amounts to $100,000. And if you pay for more than one claim, well, you can do the math!

Let's move on to pensions

On the pension side, plans have evolved to become more affordable. As previously mentioned, they've migrated away from what we used to call a defined benefit. This used to be a promise at retirement: "I promise you a pension of $1,000 a month. We determine what that's worth today, and that money has to be invested." But employers have transitioned to cheaper schemes, more like "I give you a percentage, you put it in an account, you let it compound interest, and when you're retiring, the pot of money's there and you pay yourself a pension." Those are a lot more predictable because the employer says, "I'll give you 3% or 4%."

Another way to save money, more and more companies are hiring either part-timers or consultants, as generally pension and benefits are not provided to these workers.

I've also heard people saying that as soon as they become eligible for pensions or benefits, they are being terminated. This is more common for the Generation Y. Employers just can't afford to pay benefits to maturists and boomers, and at the same time be as generous to the younger generations.

As a result, the Y-ers have never seen a decent pension plan, and the Z-ers won't either. Not only that, but they're paying for their elders too: the maturists, baby boomers, and generation X. They're paying for other people to have benefits, while their own future doesn't look bright, even though they make their required contributions.

This is how it works: while some employers pay all the benefits costs, others share the costs 50/50 with employees. So if the premium is $100 a month, then the employer pays $50, and the worker pays $50. The cost, which is commonly called the premium, is generally the same for all employees.

But an employee in the 45-plus age group probably uses $200 or $ 300 of the benefits. Meanwhile, somebody who is in the Generation Y and Z barely uses the money. So they pay $50, but they may not use $50. Obviously, this is how insurance works, similarly to social programs: We contribute to them and they pay when we need it. But it has become very onerous, very expensive and quite uneven as to who benefits versus who pays. And that, I feel, limits decent wages or the ability of the employer to increase salaries and provide proper benefits and pension.

That may be one of the reasons why many young people are willing to take more risk to start their own businesses: They don't want to rely on someone else's promises and financial schemes. They believe that "I can't expect anyone else to take care of me, so I'd better take care of myself."

This seems to point out that the old way of meeting the pension and benefits needs of multi-generational employees doesn't work any more. It's now time to stop the bleeding, so this situation doesn't keep on reproducing itself as the generations go through the workforce. And if companies do not change the way they are, the cost problems will remain and the workforce is going to keep on getting sick and be costly, while there will be no pension to help them retire. The current approaches of cost cutting, reducing or transferring costs to employees, are not the right solutions either.

Points to remember:

Five generations currently in the workforce have different expectations: While older people follow the traditional model, younger ones look for innovative ways to structure their careers, such as flexibility and shorter workdays. Throughout the generations you also have what I call the life cycle; the Xers will move from being the "Sandwich" Generation to the empty nesters in their 50s, and the Yers will become the "Sandwich" Generation, and so on.

The five age groups also have different needs for the compensation and benefits package, but currently the older workers can depend on getting their full package.

In the next chapter, we'll dig deeper into the scope of the pension and benefits problem we face right now.

CHAPTER 4:

The Scope of the Problem We Face

PENSIONS ARE SUPPOSED to provide economic security in retirement. That's why they were created at the end of the 19th century: To ensure that employees who worked hard their whole lives (as most people did in those days) were not left penniless when they retired.

The system had worked well for several generations of workers, but with the decreasing interest rates starting in the 1990s and the advent of new accounting rules in North America in 2000, many companies stopped offering defined benefit pensions, converting to less risky and more affordable defined contribution pension plans.

With the global financial crisis of 2008, companies suffered further deficits in their pension plans. It goes back to the example I gave in my Introduction of how costs of pension plans are determined today using very low interest rates. Add to that lower returns and it creates more challenges to keep a plan funded.

And this is where we are today, in the second decade of the 21st century.

The disappearing dream

Once upon a time, in the so-called "good old days," the defined benefit pension was a standard. Employers and workers both contributed to a pension plan, and the employee knew how much he would receive at retirement.

But, as already mentioned, those days are long gone (though certainly not forgotten!)

There are two reasons for this phenomenon: One, low interest rates, and two – which we already covered previously – corporate costs are soaring as retirees live longer and an aging workforce nears retirement. As a result, pension plans are more expensive to run now than they were decades ago.

Just how serious is this situation? A few years ago, International Monetary Fund (IMF) published the first empirical assessment of the impact of longevity risk on pension plans. The results show that each year of life expectancy raises pension liabilities by 3% to 4%.

Those are global figures, but what about Canada specifically? According to an article published in the Toronto Star in April of 2014, "In Canada's private sector, only one person in five has a workplace pension." This means that the vast majority of Canadians – a staggering 80% - don't have access to any type of employer-sponsored plan. And that addresses, at least in part, this chapter's title: "The Scope of the Problem We Face."

But there's more: According to a Globe and Mail report, 1.6 million Canadian seniors at the low end of the wealth scale are trying to get by on less than $15,000 a year.

Here's another angle that sheds light on the scope of this problem: Once a pension fund is established, it can't be taken away. In other words, whatever workforce a company had when it started changing its pension, it must continue to give out the benefits as they were accumulated prior to the change. Unless the company can pay out today all that has been accumulated by each participant via what we call a "windup" of the plan, this means that this big liability will stay with the company until every single current and future retiree dies. That's 30 or 40 years down the road. Or possibly more!

Yes, employers put money aside for that purpose, but the soaring costs have to be borne by the company in good times and bad (and, as we have seen, lately the times have been bad). Nowadays, the big expensive plans can easily cost the employer between 12% and 18% of payroll.

This is the situation if the company is still viable. But what happens if it goes bankrupt?

Typically, the pension plan will be terminated and its assets distributed to plan members in accordance with the plan's liabilities and pension legislation.

However, if a company goes bankrupt, the pension plan is likely underfunded, so there would not be sufficient assets to pay all accrued pension benefits. This is the worst-case scenario: workers and retirees will not receive all the pension benefits they have been promised. This has happened in the past – for instance, in the case of Nortel Networks, where both pension and post-retirement benefits had to be reduced or disappeared altogether.

In sickness and in health...

Even if a company is still alive - even if not exactly thriving – all the stresses can have a negative impact on the workforce. As I already mentioned in Chapter 2, people might have to take time off more often because they can't cope with everything that is expected of them.

Mental stress is a real problem. According to the Canadian General Social Survey (GSS), slightly more than 1 in 4 Canadian workers described their day-to-day lives as highly stressful; 62% among them identified work as their main source of stress.

I've personally seen some examples of highly stressed workers. One of my employees was losing her hair due to the excessive stress she felt at work. And of course I remedied that situation. But generally it's not at all an uncommon situation, especially in an organization that is supported by government funding. They've experienced multiple cuts and so have to do more with less, which often results in a stressed and anxious workforce.

I've also witnessed such situations in the health industry. I know, it is a paradox when health industry makes people ill, but dealing with sick people day in and day out can be nerve-wracking, especially when funding is limited for running the business.

Obviously, high levels of stress among so many employees present a challenge to both employers and the health care system. GSS report noted that mental health problems alone are estimated to cost employers about $20 billion annually and account for over three-quarters of short-term disability claims in Canada.

Coverage of prescription medication is a key component of corporate benefits packages. In the past decade, I have not seen an employer who has not budgeted an anti-depressant drug as one of his top five drugs. Then, of course, there must be a budget for other medications as well; in an aging workforce, arthritis and other conditions are very common.

On top of that, biological drugs that are being used are extremely expensive - we're talking about $30,000 to $100,000 per person. So if there's an employee who has to take a drug for the rest of his life – well, you can do the math! That will, of course, increase the cost of your plan exponentially.

Sickness and disability rate is especially high in industries where physical work is required and employees are therefore more susceptible to injuries. In case a worker gets ill in such an environment, the costs to an employer are two-fold.

First, the employer will have to pay for any medication that the sick employee needs, plus 60% to 70% of his pay. Secondly, a replacement worker may have to be hired to do the job of the missing person, so that the productivity doesn't decrease. That worker would be paid a full salary, which means the employee who is laid up costs the company big bucks, raising costs across the payroll.

Let's take an example of a large company that employs 200 people. On any given day, it's not uncommon to see 5% or even 10% of its workforce on sick leave. That's a total of 10 – 20 workers, which could add up to 30% or 40% of your pay for benefits. If the company has bought insurance for short-term absences, the insurance company would be paying for part of the incurred cost, but the corporation would still be paying for the insurance premium that allows the coverage.

Earlier, I cited a study that showed absent workers cost the Canadian economy a whooping $16.6 billion a year. Even when you divide this amount by the number of companies in Canada, the financial picture you get is pretty grim.

Crunching more numbers

Remember what happened in Greece in 2015? The country went broke and had to be bailed out by the European Union.

I know Canada is not Greece, but that country is, nevertheless, a good example of what could happen when we promise things we can't afford.

As much as you want to look after your employees, you may not be able to anymore, unless you change your approach.

We have seen how costly sickness and disability are, and this expense is not going to disappear because people will continue to get sick. The reserves have to be there, and if there are not enough, then the employer has to fund them, increasing their payment to the insurance company.

Employers usually pay through premium increases, but those are significant. It's not as uncommon anymore to see disability take a hike in their renewals of anywhere between 30% and 50% in premium increase. That's tremendous.

Of course, there is always a possibility of negotiations between the employer and insurance company. But insurance companies are businesses and can't run on deficits. If they go belly-up, then nobody will be paying for benefits. That's not something we want to see happen.

Although insurance companies are in the business of selling, well yes, *insurance,* sometimes it doesn't work that way. At times, they could feel like saying to an employer: "You're way too big of a liability. We're going to cut you."

Even in the insurance industry, business decisions can be justified from a purely financial point of view. Sometimes, they have to address difficult situations with a client, and unless the carrier can help the client recover, they may have to tell them that they're not going to renew their benefits. It's not happening yet, but it might happen in the future. Benefits are not required by law. Unlike in the case of a pension, if you do give a pension, there are minimums you have to abide by, but you don't *have to* give a pension.

There are no such rules for benefits like life insurance, disability or drugs either. You can offer benefits, but it's not an obligation. If an insurance company said, "Well, sorry. We're going to have to terminate your disability plan," then the client that is being "fired" will have to turn around and find another carrier to take them on. That will be very costly, as the new carrier will consider the client's past claim history. No insurance company is going to take your risk on and not check what has happened in the past.

I am not aware of this happening, yet. Currently, insurance companies will just increase your premiums to the level they feel they need to cover your claims. This may look like a firing in disguise, as you might not be able to pay for the premiums. So you'll want to go to market to check if you can move to another carrier. The risk is that no one can propose an affordable premium to you. Bottom line: Your sick employees are expensive!

I'm not an expert on the intricacies of closing your disability plan. As mentioned, there are reserves set aside to pay for benefits but at the time of termination, they may not be sufficient to cover the remaining claims. There will therefore be compromises; possibly the amount of disability provided for the individuals on disability will be reduced to what the reserves can afford. And, of course, no new cases will be added on as the plan is closed to new employees. As an example, when Nortel Networks went bankrupt, their disabled employees received lump sums of 35% of the value of what they would normally get if their payments continued until retirement (age 65).

No employer and no employee wants to hear this because it means if a worker gets sick, he'll have to go on unemployment. And that is going to create another pressure on society. I think we're getting to the point where some things have to happen.

You see this situation with school boards. Their budgets are very limited and constantly decreasing. In order to avoid giving benefits to employees, they are hired on contract or they ensure that workers don't exceed a certain level of seniority that would give them benefits and pension. They just can't afford it.

Generally, with sufficient notice, companies can legally terminate their benefits. I think it's going to start happening across the board, in both public and private sectors.

Now that you've read about the possible "gloom and doom scenarios," the question is, what can be done to avoid such traumatic situations?

There definitely is a way to solve this crisis, and I'll go into more details and discuss some strategies later on in this book. For now, here are some steps you, the employer, can focus on:

- Step #1: Take a look at reality. This problem really is here; you have all five generations in the workforce and their needs are all different.

- Step #2: The solution doesn't have to be painful, but it is a major shift from what we are used to doing. It will ensure though affordability of the programs.

- Step #3: You need to create a solution that can deliver on its promises and also is adaptable to the changes of the times, the workforce and the culture.

- Step #4: Find a new way to create engagement, which is based on the needs of the workforce. It does really come from management. If people aren't overly stressed and not wanting to be at work, then they likely will come to work.

- Step #5: Capitalize on the strength of the happy employees from all generations and create a thriving organization.

Toward a non-standard employment

Clearly, we are not on the right path right now. Instead of adapting to the new realities, we are still stuck on old ways. We're patching up the symptom, not curing the underlying problem. The consequences of this short-sightedness will be grave: We are going to see more cuts in benefits, and we're also going to see companies closing their doors, and organizations being shut down by government.

Another thing that could happen – that is happening already, as a matter of fact – is that more and more companies will replace retiring or leaving employees with independent contractors. The big advantage for employers is that there are no costs, other than wages, associated with contract workers – no pension or benefits.

According to the *Pulse Survey*, which is used by companies to measure their operations and performance, 63% of HR professionals have seen an increase in the number of contract workers employed by their organizations. More than 40% of respondents said they expected this number to increase. This particular survey was carried out in 2012, so we can only imagine that the trend has consolidated since then.

Now, there's good news and bad news about this development. Let's start with the bad: Obviously, regular employees who have worked long and hard for a company will see the benefits they had depended on for years disappear.

The good news is that the non-conventional forms of employment like contract work will suit younger generations who, as I mentioned before, value flexibility and work-life balance that they can't necessarily get from full-time, permanent employment.

What about the impact on organizations? The truth is that – for all the reasons I outlined above - the only companies that will be viable are the ones that will not be paying people enough and will not be providing benefits. Yes, it sounds crazy and inhumane, but, unfortunately, that's the way things are right now.

Points to remember:

Low interest rates and low returns on investment linked to the slow global economy are now compounding the problems for pension systems, already burdened by the needs of multi-generational workforce.

Organizations have to find NEW ways to stay viable, make money, and ensure that their employees get the benefits they need and deserve.

Management *can* create a happy work environment where the people are rewarded for their strengths. We'll dig into each one of those and show how the C suite can really turn things around.

In the next chapter, we'll get specific: We'll explore the reality of your organization. Stay tuned!

CHAPTER 5:

The Reality in Organizations Today

IN THE PREVIOUS chapters, we talked about the pension and benefits-related challenges that many employers are facing today: There is just not enough money to ensure that the younger generations presently in the workforce will be able to depend on those payouts.

Now let's focus on the situation in your organization. Where do you stand on the issue? And later on in the chapter I'll suggest some money-saving corrections and adjustments you can make.

The challenges you face

When was the last time you examined your pension and benefits plan to see whether it needed restructuring? And have you actually given any thought to what measures should be taken to achieve that goal?

If so, you are far from the only one to recognize that something needs to be done. A number of firms across Canada in both public and private sectors are either considering or already implementing various measures. This is not surprising, because in the 1970s, 10% of payroll went towards pension and benefits and today that number is 30% to 50%. That's an enormous burden for organizations to bear.

One example of the restructure is Canada Post. As reported by CBC in July 2016, "While promising to keep the status quo for existing plan members, Canada Post wants to switch the company's pension plan from a defined benefit plan, to a defined contribution one."

The article went on to explain why Canada Post had to implement those drastic changes: "Its pension is a behemoth, but even not immune to broader forces in the investment world. Persistently low interest rates are problematic for pension plans, because they depress the returns that funds rely on to stay on top of their obligations."

Basically, Canada Post's problems were not that different from those experienced by other companies, both big and small. The important thing to know is this: There are some quick fixes that can be made. But ultimately, you should be creating a plan for longer-term sustainable change.

This may sound like an impossible task, but it isn't. Fact is, any organization can implement cost reduction measures with some simple strategies, good management skills, and a flexible mindset.

Customizing work hours

First thing to consider is the workforce breakdown in your organization: Not just the generations, but also life cycles because even though we tie a generation to a person, they will evolve through the ages as well. Generation Z is not going to remain in their early 20s forever. They're going to be moving towards the ages of the X and the Y.

Nowadays, 20-somethings are usually having children later. This means they are flexible and will give you a lot of their time, if needed. That may not be the case with 30-somethings, who likely have young kids and family obligations (remember the Sandwich Generation?), so they'll be focused on managing the work-life balance. This is going to pose a lot of problems in terms of how engaged they are at work and how stressed out they may become.

Not surprisingly, the 35 to 45 age group has the most stress-related ailments - they consume the lion's share of antidepressants and take most of the sick leaves. Those are extremely common challenges in that age group, something that the employer has to deal with.

And if your workforce includes maturists and boomers, you're likely to have arthritis cases, or other age-related health conditions, all of which probably require medications. You're still accumulating pension for them, and those pension costs are quite extreme.

It's important to know the demographics of your workforce and to manage the needs of each age group. And that is where your willingness to make some adjustments and accommodate these needs is so important.

So what can you do? I believe that respecting the life cycles would be key in reducing costs. For instance, if you have employees who are in their 20s and who have lots of time and no family obligations, ask them to work more hours. Chances are, they'll be happy to oblige. Or they might not. More and more studies, and everyone I talk to about the new generations, usually tell me that the new employees are not keen on working long hours.

Now, if you have people working more hours and ensuring productivity, you can afford to be more accommodating with the 30 and 40-somethings who may even forego income to have a more flexible work schedule.

Or, you might have the 20-something workers who have young families, while the employees in their 30s are childless and those in their 40s are empty nesters.

There too, you can adapt to their expectations. The key here is flexibility, which provides a choice to employees as to how they can deliver their work. The flexibility will help employees feel trusted that they could deliver their work based on their own schedule. They will be more satisfied and happier.

There is plenty of anecdotal evidence and some research too that show a correlation between happiness and productivity. For instance, the Corporate Executive Board, a global best practice insights and technology company, which represents 80% of the Fortune 500 companies, researched 500,000 workers around the world and found that employees who have good work-life balance work harder than those who don't.

And, it goes without saying that hard working employees are more productive, and productivity, in turn, leads to the good bottom line. So it's a win-win situation.

Bending the rules

Another solution you might want to consider implementing is telecommuting – having your employees work from home, using the Internet, e-mail, and the telephone.

Now, your first reaction to this suggestion may be, "If I don't supervise my workers and have no control over what they are doing, they will slack off."

Actually, that's not very likely to happen. Just like with a reduced-hours model, home-based employees can be as (if not more) efficient as their colleagues on the work site.

A number of studies show that telecommuting actually *boosts* productivity and performance. One of them, The Remote Collaborative Worker Survey released in 2015, reported the following findings: Of those who worked remotely at least a few times per month, 77% noticed greater productivity while working offsite; 30% said they accomplished more in less time; and 24% said they accomplished more in the same amount of time.

One example of such forward-thinking company is Export Development Canada (EDC), which is a Crown corporation. They moved buildings a few years ago, and they told their staff that, on any given day, they would only be able to accommodate about

60% of their workforce in the workplace. So that would mean that some people would have to work from home.

Surprisingly, when the new building was ready, there was enough room to have a desk for everyone! EDC still maintained its new policy allowing flexibility in where their employees preferred to work.

Great stories to hear; a woman I know was able to accompany her spouse on a small business trip, still work her normal hours, and she didn't have to hide that fact!

On its website, EDC says: "We make every effort to ensure that your career and life are kept in balance. We offer telework and flexible work arrangements, including flexible hours, compressed workweeks and part-time schedules, when possible."

It's true that telecommuting may not appeal to everyone – for whatever reasons. Maybe some employees prefer the social interaction of a workplace to the solitude (or maybe distractions) of their homes, or perhaps they feel they are not organized or disciplined enough to be productive offsite.

But studies show the opposite trend: Long-term market research by International Data Corporation Canada found that, by 2016, 73% of Canadians are doing at least some remote work.

The chart below clearly shows this trend:

Majority of Gen Y Workers Would Like to Be Able to Work From Home

(share of full-time, employed Canadian survey respondents who would be much/somewhat more satisfied, by age, per cent)

  ░ Working remotely

  ■ Using cloud software allowing access to work information from home

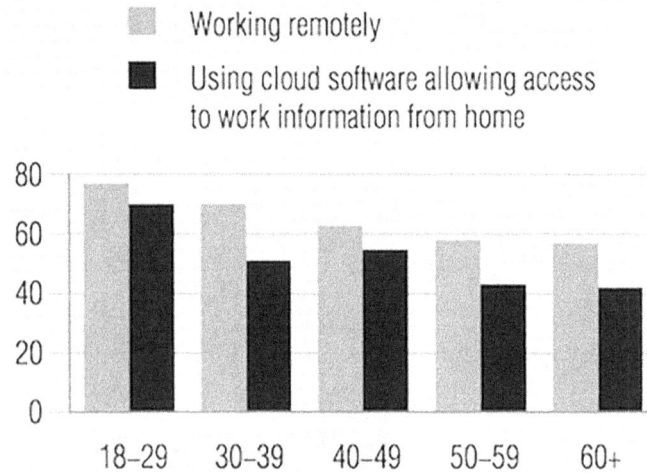

Note: Respondents were asked if being able to work remotely and using cloud software to work from home would increase their job satisfaction.
Source: Rogers Communications and Harris/Decima, *Rogers Innovation Report: Connected Workplace.*

For employees, telecommuting is about a better work-life balance. For employers, the financial benefits are significant: Lower overhead, reduced absenteeism and turnover, and increased productivity.

But there's more: According to an article published in Huffington Post in June 2016, "The number of benefits companies enjoy with a remote workforce are impressive and far-reaching."

The article refers to a WORKshift Canada report, "The Bottom Line on Telework," which demonstrates that employers can save over $10,000 per year for every employee who telecommutes only two days each week.

Those are all compelling reasons to re-think the traditional work models and adopt a more open approach to employment practices.

The elephant in the room

Why then do we see companies today going back to office work, and why are there so many employers saying no to flexible hours for different generations, or less hours for one vs the other? Because the management style has not adapted to the new reality.

One of the worst things I have seen in any workplace is how employees watch over each other and count their colleagues' hours, monitor their comings and goings, without really having any facts as to their work productivity. In addition, too many managers consider an employee working from home under the category of "absenteeism. " This potentially goes back to the older days where you actually had to walk over to someone's desk to talk to them.

Therefore the thinking is that if you are not sitting at your desk, you are not working. Haven't they heard of "presenteeism?"

This is a sad state of affairs in the corporate world; employees watching over each other and complaining about each other. And it highly jeopardizes the success of strategies I propose that will give back employees some flexibility and trust to do their jobs.

I, for one, have struggled with this all of my corporate career. Being an innovator, strategist, and networker, I couldn't always do my job sitting at my desk. But my achievements being out there — connecting, fostering relationships with clients or suppliers, finding solutions to our current challenges at hand — didn't seem to have value for my superior. And based on my job description, I had the mandate to do what I was doing, I had the title of executive next to my name and I was responsible for managing costs. Instead, I was expected to stay at my desk and wait for calls from my superior... That is how it felt: that I was there to be available for whatever my superior wanted me to do; not what I thought I needed to do. It always made me wonder why I was even there, why they hired me in the first place. I did not feel like I had any authority or power to do my job. Over the years I have heard numerous such stories, with the underlying reality that employees did not feel they were trusted to do their job and they did not have any flexibility as to how to get the job done.

And this is where management can really fail; if you cannot embrace and openly tell your employees: "I trust you, and you are expected to do your job because you want to and you are looking to contribute to something. The competition is not with your peers, but with yourself."

Like at Crew Labs, Stephanie Liverani's employment contract is in plain English; it summarizes the job and requests best efforts to achieve a workload goal that will require teamwork. There are no fixed hours mentioned - just the annual compensation, the employee's responsibilities, and a minimum guaranteed vacation time of three weeks' vacation. But if someone wants more, the corporate culture is to never refuse.

Now even though Crew Labs is in the modern IT industry, reread the paragraph above and tell me realistically if it cannot fit most office jobs. Too many employment contracts are outdated, never rewritten, and basically a one-way agreement in the favor of the employer.

Fostering a happy workforce

Let's talk more about the link between employee satisfaction and increased productivity, especially as it pertains to cost-saving measures.

What happens when an employee is out sick? Such absences carry hidden costs: Replacement workers and overtime charges raise costs. In the previous chapter we did the math: First, the employer will have to pay for any medication that the sick employee needs, plus 60% to 70% of his pay. Secondly, a replacement worker may have to be hired to do the job of the missing person, so that the productivity doesn't decrease. That worker would be paid a full salary, which means the employee who is laid up costs the company big bucks, raising costs across the payroll.

It is therefore logical that keeping the workers healthy is a big money saver.   In short-term disability I mentioned that three quarters of cases are due to some mental health related problems. In long-term disability, mental health is the cause of 40% or more cases.   And in almost 100% of the cases, the work environment is identified as the main cause of the disability.

So how do you, as an employer, achieve the healthy and productive workplace? The answer is two-fold: One, create an environment that will minimize the incidence of illness and, therefore, associated costs. And two, create an environment where your employees are motivated and engaged, boosting productivity and bottom line.

To ensure a happy and healthy workforce, some big companies like Google and Facebook offer their employees on-site recreational facilities and other benefits. As Google notes on its website, "We want

Googlers to be happy and healthy both inside and outside of work. Our benefits and perks vary by region, but they're all based on the philosophy that taking care of our people is good for all of us. We know that everyone is different, so what we offer is constantly evolving based on employee needs and feedback."

Your organization may not have the resources to provide such amenities, but you can certainly deliver on the promise in the last line: "We know that everyone is different, so what we offer is constantly evolving based on employee needs and feedback." This is why knowing the age breakdown of your workforce and understanding its needs is so important. But don't forget that flexibility is key and you have to provide as many choices as possible in how your workforce delivers its output. Only by making changes that actually take into consideration what your employees' needs and wants are, will you be successful.

Here are some of the performance boosting, cost-saving strategies to implement in your company:

Strategy #1: Be flexible and open. If an employee asks to reduce his or her hours and it is feasible for you to do, then accommodate that request. Remember: a worker who is not stressed out is a worker who may not get sick as often and cost you less in the end. Mathematically, there is no reason you can't adjust the individual's hours. You can adjust their pay to correspond to the new hours; although some benefits may remain the same as for full time employees. But it has been proven that workers will be healthier and likely not cost you as much anyway. What message does that send to others? That you are a flexible and adaptable employer who is able to understand in specific conditions of your employees. This strategy works even better when you look at rewriting your HR policies around work hours and productivity, as well when you rewrite your employment contract. Like in the Crew Labs example, you make it a mutually satisfactory contract between two parties, as opposed to a one-way set of rules and regulations.

Strategy #2: A number of studies have shown that performance and productivity are not related to the number of hours worked. Researchers at the OECD, for example, have discovered an interesting link between how much people work and how productive they are: Working longer hours actually results in a *reduction* of output. If your culture boasts that more hours are better, it needs to stop. Rather promote productive hours so your employees can go on to other parts of their lives that they value and thrive in. Also promote healthy lifestyle by reminding your employees that they need their sleep. Sleep your way to a successful career as Arianna Huffington recommends in her book *Thrive*.

Strategy #3: Building on Strategy number 1. Get rid of the employment contract that dictates hours you need to work. Many types of work are measurable as to their productivity. I was once told that in sales you could not work less than full time. That does not add up for me. You tell your employee, "You are expected to sell X amount of this product. I don't care how long it takes, but you need to do that, and there's an incentive for you to sell more." This would go a long way to creating a sense of trust and empowerment because the employee is given a goal but he or she can choose how to achieve it. (And it also ties in with Strategy #2, assessing your employees in terms of results, rather than hours).

If you practice these strategies in your organization, you will be able to reduce your sick pay and insurance costs. At the same time, you'll get a huge bonus: an increase in performance, productivity, staff morale, and employee engagement. You just have to listen to what your employees need, want, and what are they complaining about in the workplace.

Points to remember:

Successful long-term cost-cutting measures can be fairly simple and require little or no financial investment. They are mostly a matter of adjusting some management practices and customizing work hours to the needs of various age and life cycle groups in the workforce.

Fostering a healthy environment is a sound cost-slashing strategy, as it will boost worker productivity and, subsequently, the bottom line.

In the next chapter, we will look at how this shifts from the more common approaches to cost cutting.

CHAPTER 6:

The Major Shift in our Way of Finding Solutions

FOLLOWING UP ON the last chapter, your organization has to face the reality of the increasing costs of your pension and benefits plan. It's getting harder and harder to pay for it, and it's becoming too expensive to sustain.

That's why you have to make sure you find a way to manage these costs. The programs and the benefits plans that fit another generation or another time won't apply anymore. If we don't change this, the reality of the times will change it for us.

Climbing costs

As noted previously, in the 1970s, 10% of payroll went towards pension and benefits; today, that number is 30% to 50%. That's the situation right now and the percentage will continue to soar.

Fact is – and we covered this before – that employee benefits cost a lot of money. As noted, the average annual cost to a company of providing benefits, not including pension costs, is $8,330 per full-time employee, according to a survey by the Conference Board of Canada.

As a result, many employers are looking for new ways to keep their organizations financially sustainable. Many are changing their pension plans to more predictable and cheaper ones – for instance, as outlined previously, Canada Post is planning to switch the company's pension plan from a defined benefit plan, to a defined contribution one. Other companies are transferring benefits costs onto employees. That's because benefits represent a significant investment for employers, which they can no longer afford, for all the reasons mentioned before: low interest rates on investments and an aging workforce, increase in mental health issues and other illnesses, and growing use of more sophisticated drugs, driving up health premiums.

Much of this re-shuffling is coming down to a shift in responsibility. The old mentality among employees was, "I can just work for this company and it will take care of my health, my life, my retirement, and everything. I don't have to do anything." That thinking no longer applies to the current reality. Now, the employers are saying, "I can't survive with these costs. I'm being crippled in my revenue."

In Chapter 5, I outlined some suggestions on how organizations can cut their costs while still fostering a healthy and motivated workforce. Among the strategies I laid out was implementation of flexible work hours, as well as telecommuting, both of which can help companies save money through lower overhead and reduced absenteeism, while boosting employee performance and productivity.

These are proven cost-cutting measures, saving tens of thousands of dollars per year and per employee.

Safety in numbers

It is always difficult to make significant changes with blind faith that they will achieve what you are hoping for: increased productivity and revenue while costs are kept under control. Therefore, many of the solutions today focus on reducing and managing costs. Consulting services that you may hire will analyze your costs, your employees' consumption habits of benefits. and look for ways to better control these costs in the future. Those are tangible and comfortable results of expensive analyses that you may have requested.

I did those exercises at Canada Post and we designed a drug formulary that really helped curtail rising costs that were coming in the pipeline. The cost of drugs is still a major problem today as plans continue to see double-digit increases in their health plans.

Among the main factors driving up the cost are biologic medications that are being routinely prescribed; they are the most expensive drugs in Canada, costing about $30,000 to $100,000 per person. So if there's an employee who has to take this medication for the rest of his life, the cost of the healthcare plan will increase dramatically. Even traditional (non-biological) drugs are very costly. When a medication is developed it is referred to as a brand name drug and it is protected by a patent for a certain number of years. During this time, the manufacturer recaptures the costs of research and development of such drugs.

To manage these costs without cutting employees' health benefits, many organizations have ensured that their plans cover the generic equivalent of the brand name drug, when it becomes available. The generic drugs; on average, will cost 60% less than the brand-name medications, so that's a considerable saving right there.

Here's an example of price discrepancies: According to a 2015 CBC report, a brand-name cholesterol lowering drug, Lipitor (10mg/90 pills), sells in Canada for $168.83, while the generic equivalent, Atorvastatin, costs only $28.24.

Some of the most common health conditions, including high cholesterol, depression, allergies, and diabetes, have generic medications available. And if all the employees who can switch to generics do so, then your savings on healthcare costs can be significant.

Savings due to design tweaking as just outlined above are already a common reality for many employers. If your company hasn't yet switched to this cost control mechanism, it is easy to do so. But for the ones that have, their costs are still going up yearly. Some employers would also prefer not forcing any cost containing design changes to their plan as they like their workers to have choice. In any event, you can only do so much in cutting costs. At the end of the day, you still have sick employees.

And these options we just looked at also do not address the increase in absenteeism due to illness or surges in the incidence and cost of long-term disability.

The benefits of prevention

Another very common trend now that has proven to be also a very effective way to cut your healthcare costs is investing in a wellness program in your company.

You might be thinking," *Invest?* But I have no money for such things; I want to *cut* costs, not increase the spending!". And there is the uncomfortable reality that you don't know if you are going to recover those costs somehow or this is just a way to give something to your employees.

A few years ago, Rand Corporations published a study called "Do Workplace Wellness Programs Save Employers Money?" It examined 10 years of data and concluded that disease management delivered 86% of the hard healthcare costs, generated $136 in savings per employee each month, and a 30% reduction in hospital admissions. This study shows that the biggest savings are in managing the sick employees. And the savings are not necessarily for just the organization. In Canada the beneficiary is the social program, not the employer. While this is great news and wellness/prevention programs are a positive addition to any workplace, it will not save you the costs that you are really trying to control. Not as much as what I will propose to do.

The Rand study concludes three things:

1. "If an employer wants to improve employee health or productivity, an evidence-based lifestyle management program can achieve this goal. But employers who are seeking a healthy

ROI on their programs should target employees who already have chronic diseases."

2. "Second, given the lack of financial return from the lifestyle component, employers need to pay attention to cost." The disease management which may include one-on-one consulting can be very expensive.

3. "Third, execution really matters. The findings presented here are derived from leading employers with a strong organizational commitment to wellness and substantial experience with running programs. Learning from them how to engage employees and achieve fundamental behavior change would be prudent for employers who want comparable results."

You might have considered wellness programs for your organization, and possibly implemented some. However, it's not necessarily the people you think should use the wellness program that will do so. That's probably one of the flaws behind it, because the weight loss programs for seriously overweight employees may not be used by those people but rather by the slightly overweight ones.

Another example is stress reduction. You can't just assume that one stress-reduction model is going to work for everyone in your workplace. At the

Huffington Post, they actually put in place meditation sessions and meditation rooms where people
could learn to meditate and practice meditation.
That worked very well for that type of industry and
was shown to reduce hugely the level of stress, and
even create a big increase in productivity. But this
particular organization is doing something more
than just programs like meditation rooms; they have
a very healthy work environment in general.

And that is what my solution focuses on, which
is also the third finding of the Rand study — for
the programs to be successful, it matters how your
organization approaches workplace wellness. This is
where I see the real potential that has barely been
tapped into:

**Wellness programs are addressing the
symptoms that are apparent; employees are not
healthy, they are stressed, and they are getting
sick. But the deeply-rooted problems remain and
you are only achieving some of the rewards.**

Sadly, any unhealthy workplace can offer programs such as indicated above, while still limiting its
fuller potential of a really healthy environment. My
solution is simpler than programs, although it can be
harder to fully understand and implement.

For your organization to be really successful, you
need to re-design your employment offering. This

will require two main things: first, your perception of what it is to be the employer—the ultimate decision maker, and an authority-type manager. Secondly, your employees' perception and expectation to be looked after by you, as long as they abide by all your rules and follow your lead.

Employees will also need to change their perception of you as an employer; you are no longer there to look after them, or at least should not be expected to. And it is more perception than reality. Both employers and employees are subconsciously keeping the old-style workplace expectations alive and kicking:

1. You can't really work efficiently for less than 40 hours a week; even though today you have the very powerful tool that is the computer to facilitate your job;

2. A manager needs to know where his/her employees are at all times; they are to be in the office;

3. Employees perceive their bosses as the ones in charge, the position is one of control over employees; ultimately deciding everything.

4. Managers behave like they have all the answers and make all the decisions because they have the position of authority.

5. My superior/boss owns my time, owns me when I am at work. I do what I am told, not what I think I should do.

I am paraphrasing what I have seen over and over in my career, the typical corporate structure and what the model is like everywhere.

Hiring someone has now become a process, very mechanical, with not too many discussions around what the relationship is to be like between the employee and the manager.

How do you feel after going through the five statements above? Are you hyped and ready to do the job? Do you feel energized that your opinion and your contribution will matter? Will you feel engaged? On its website, Aon Hewitt writes this about employee engagement: "Low employee engagement is pervasive—nearly half of the world's employees are not engaged. Our research across more than 7,000 organizations indicates that each disengaged employee costs your organization an average of $10,000 in profit annually. Can you afford this hidden expense?"

I'll talk about this subject further later on, but in the meantime consider this: disengaged workers cost money in many ways, including in absenteeism and in benefits, because disengagement leads to unhappiness, stress, and often to mental health issues. Whether you believe this to be true or not, engaging your employees properly will not only save you in benefit costs but it will also increase productivity, because engaged employees are productive employees:

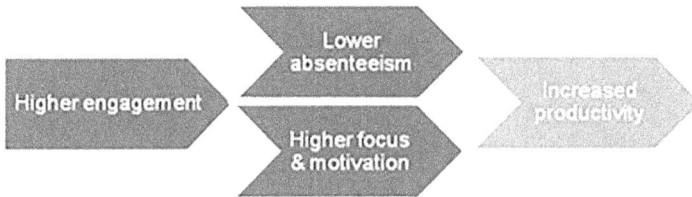

Points to remember:

In this chapter, I got into the heart of what my solution is all about: attacking the source of the problem as opposed to managing the costs of the symptoms. There is a lot more that you can do to manage your cost by simply taking a fresh look at how you are treating your employees. As we spend so much of our day at work, if we cannot realize ourselves there and feel that we have some control over our time at work, then our health will suffer. Our engagement will diminish, we will just go through the motions, and we will cost our employer more money in the process.

In the next chapter, we will talk further about creating solutions that deliver on promises, adapt to changes, and really address the problem rather than the symptoms.

CHAPTER 7:

The Solution Must Deliver On Promises & Adapt To Changes

THE WORKPLACE OF today has very little resemblance to the workplace of the 20th century. The work and economic environments also keep evolving. There is a need to adapt to current realities to address the cost pressures coming from the pension and benefits provided to employees.

Generally, the first thing that companies will do is look at reducing costs, because it's never popular to increase the price of your product. They'll cut costs in either their operating expenses or the benefits or the pension. In turn, what does that do to employees? It really minds their engagement and their feeling of belonging and dedication to an employer, as they are losing something. They're paying for the fluctuations. Then you factor in the changing workforce, with different needs that are not met for the different generations and life cycles.

The solution is to change the workplace. I am not proposing that organizations cut pension and benefits altogether, or keep reducing them. Instead, employers need to work with employees to create a new work proposition where the usage will decrease naturally. The benefits will be there for the catastrophic situations. Not everybody can predict that they won't have cancer, diabetes or other ailments. Their illnesses or mental health issues are not necessarily workplace-related.

Catastrophic coverage is really important to have. Ideally employees shouldn't need them to just cope with life. Right now for example, there's a record number of people on mental health medication. Research shows that mental problems are quite prevalent; in Canada in 2012, 1 in 3 Canadians (about 9.1 million people), met the criteria for at least one of the six selected mental or substance use disorders at some point in their lives, according to Statistics Canada. The six selected disorders are: depression (major depressive episode), bipolar disorder, general anxiety disorder; alcohol, cannabis or other substances abuse or dependence make up the last three.

The big question is why mental health issues are the main contributors to costs of benefits? Simply, we just cannot cope.

In a newer model, in a different workplace, where employees are actually happy at work and are fulfilled, we will see a decrease in the use of benefits. Currently as employees are burnt out and stressed out, they are experiencing more mental or substance use disorders than before. What else has changed, or should I say hasn't changed, so significantly that would explain this rise in occurrences? What other common denominator do you see that explains why there is so much more need for mental health support?

It is time for employers to change their employment contract with their employees. Employees as well have to change their expectations of their employer. It's no longer a handshake, "I'm going to look after you and your family all the way into retirement."

The Retirement Promise

The new retirement promise may include some funds put aside in a pension plan but also support employees with the tools to properly figure out what they need to retire. At the end of the day, they will be responsible for the "saving gap".

That's the foundation of my pension solution. An employer provides what he can offer or, at least, the means to figure it out. In other words, when it comes to pensions, employees have to take accountability and cannot expect that the employers are there to hold their hand and look after them.

Although there is a lot of information provided around retirement, the programs are currently missing the mark: too much time is focused on explaining what the pension plan provides and not enough time spent on specific personalized details. At the end of the seminar on retirement, the same questions likely remain: The employee has a better sense of what the plan provides for but doesn't know if it is enough, and what net sum will be in his pocket when all is all said and done (taking into account income taxes and any other possible deductions).

Retirement support I am suggesting is to start with what each employee thinks he needs as income to live in retirement

When I looked at my own retirement planning a few months ago, I was thrilled to find out that all I needed to do was something quite simple and I could adapt and realize my retirement plan.

It's usually common near one's 40's to start thinking, "Okay, well, I need to make sure I have enough money for retirement."

So as indicated, all employee first need to figure out what proportion of their income that they are earning today they would still need once retired. And that is done by looking at current expenses that would still have to be paid after retirement. For example, let's say today, you determine that your monthly expenses are $5,000. Then you figure that because you won't have a mortgage (or you hope you won't have a mortgage), and your last child will be soon leaving the nest, you can probably live on $3,500. So that's what your retirement goal is; you need $3,500 a month at retirement, in order to live adequately. And to keep it simple, let's keep it in today's dollars.

Now you need to pick a realistic retirement date, taking into account that you will live much longer and likely healthier than your parents and predecessors. You can also take into consideration working part time.

A financial advisor can do this very simply - once he or she knows your target monthly income for retirement and an approximate retirement age, he can figure out if what you have saved up to now and what you're planning to save will be sufficient. She can also take into account the value of any properties you may have, any pension plans with current or former employers, and what the Canadian Pension Plan will pay you out. Maybe you're also putting money in a Registered Retirement Savings Plan (RRSP) in Canada or a 401K in the US. Once all the current information is provided, the advisor will figure out what your gap is today.

I did different calculations myself, and I included a worst-case scenario, where I wanted to fully retire at age 65. For that scenario, I was missing just a few $100 a month that I needed to save. And that, to me, was great news, as opposed to realizing, "Oh, we're in big trouble." Without going through the exercise, I was going to, like many other people, blindly save way more than that, and even constantly worry about how much I'd need.

Of course, with my background, I can calculate my expected retirement income and possible gap myself; I understand the mathematics behind it. But how difficult is it for everyone else who does not have any background in the field? How are they supposed to figure out what they need for retirement?

Many people have a fear or live in that unknown. They don't know where to go for help. This is a need that employers can address. Instead of just throwing money in a pension plan and hope for the best, they can help their employees figure out where they are at with their savings, what they need to retire, and how they are going to get to their goal. That is the real gap to fill. Not everyone will have the same need at retirement. The industry is reconsidering actually the whole concept of determining what is needed after retirement as a percentage of your pre-retirement earnings; like the 60% I mentioned in a previous chapter. The answer varies per individual and it is highly dependent on each person's situation, current savings, and expected spending at retirement.

This approach to educating employees to plan their own retirement can be very empowering and gratifying; not only will employees know when they can retire but also how much income they will need and have. Employees are now made responsible and accountable for their own retirement.

The most organizations do today is provide tools to employees to project to retirement. That is not sufficient. I would even boldly go to the extent of recommending that Human Resources should have specialist(s) — individual(s) who will have to ensure all employees are fully aware of how to determine their retirement goal and what they need to save. That is an employment promise that can be kept.

Human Resources Reinvented

The employees value things that aren't necessarily money. Numerous studies out there demonstrate that the majority of employees do not stay at a job only for financial rewards. Just look at this chart from Harvard Business Review:

WHAT EMPLOYEES VALUE AT WORK

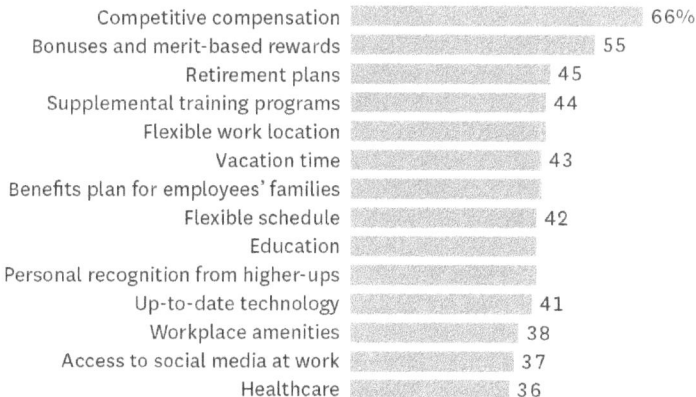

Competitive compensation	66%
Bonuses and merit-based rewards	55
Retirement plans	45
Supplemental training programs	44
Flexible work location	
Vacation time	43
Benefits plan for employees' families	
Flexible schedule	42
Education	
Personal recognition from higher-ups	
Up-to-date technology	41
Workplace amenities	38
Access to social media at work	37
Healthcare	36

Furthermore, there are many studies that show that one of the main reasons that employees leave their job is because of their bosses, not money. People leave a company primarily because of the management style that they are under. As you can see in this chart, more than 40% of employees quit their jobs precisely for that reason:

Top reasons why people left their old job:

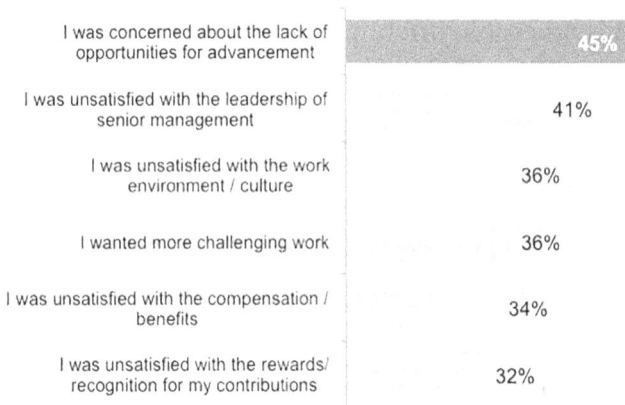

I was concerned about the lack of opportunities for advancement	45%
I was unsatisfied with the leadership of senior management	41%
I was unsatisfied with the work environment / culture	36%
I wanted more challenging work	36%
I was unsatisfied with the compensation / benefits	34%
I was unsatisfied with the rewards/ recognition for my contributions	32%

What about staying and facing the situation at hand? Where does one get assistance to deal with an unhealthy work environment? Usually it is Human Resources. Let's take a closer look at what a HR department really does: it ensures that corporate policies are observed and that everyone embraces the culture in place, just the way it is. That everyone conforms. There is no place for the employee's advocate; no one in the company is really looking after the employees and their well-being in a global way, or worries about the employee work experience.

Many of us are convinced that there has to be a policing structure around us in order to ensure that employees behave. We have to have rules, otherwise, employees take advantage, won't work their full hours, will take more time off than they are allowed. This very structure is killing engagement, productivity, and creativity, and your employees' health at the same time.

There is a benefit to having guidelines to allow for order and, like in society, the majority abides by guidelines; sadly, the authoritative management model that is so prevalent right now lacks trust towards employees and their willingness to follow the guidelines in the workplace.

There will come a time when employers will have no choice but to change the workplace to ensure engagement. Actually, there are companies that are already there – I mentioned some of them in previous chapters. A healthy workplace is no longer just a nice perk but the cost of not having one will run companies into the ground.

Increases that you are experiencing in the benefits you provide add to your cost of operation. Every dollar that you increase on there, is deducted from your revenue. And there is no additional revenue made from the spending, which means you are automatically losing profit.

Ultimately, just by following what I am suggesting in this book, employers can avoid this cycle and get themselves out of the tough spot where they would have to really struggle with operating costs in the long run. Or they'll have to choose either to stop operation or just cut more benefits and risk having a sicker workforce. It may mean some hard decisions. But remember that whatever you invest in improving your workplace, your investment will be returned in the long term. You will recover your money in multiples.

I see that the hardest part for employers to do, the most difficult decisions, will be to think out of the box and to accept that the old mentality must be replaced with the new ideas and actions — new approach, fresh eyes on how are we managing our workforce. The challenge is to develop a culture that needs to embrace the current employees, taking into account the technology influence as well as the life cycles and generational influences in the workforce.

Points to remember:

To sum up, the solution must deliver on promises are made in the context of today. We have to take care of our workforce, and our solution needs to be responsive to the people that are coming into the workforce. By focusing on creating a healthy and engaged workplace, an employer will be able to sustain its promises and deliver on them.

If you are in a really bad place where you cannot control your workforce costs anymore, you really don't have a choice but to consider this solution. You need to look at developing a leadership that is based on needs of the workforce. That will really turn your costs around; by first creating engagement, which will see your productivity go up and your costs go down.

In the following chapter, we will discuss how to create leadership and engagement based on the needs of the workforce. This will mean a revamping of the Human Resources approach and of course retraining management.

CHAPTER 8:

Leadership Based On The Needs Of The Workforce Creates Engagement

IN THIS CHAPTER we'll explore how having a better understanding of your employees, their struggles, their obligations, their needs, and even their desires outside of work, makes it much easier to manage them at work. Respecting and supporting these people's dreams and goals will have a significant impact on their performance at work.

Let's focus on the ways to increase efficiency and engagement at work by appreciating your employees and treating them well. If you create a happy and healthy work environment, everybody wins.

Currently, management is basically seen as the authority; there are organizational rules to abide by and if employees step out of line, they'll be in trouble. On the other hand, if they keep their nose to the grindstone and just go about their job, they're not going to suffer negative consequences.

Work is also seen as a source of conflict and stress, with many workers having to find a difficult balance between the requirements and expectations of the workplace and personal needs.

For example, we are constantly told to be healthy. But if you work full time, how are you going to find time to visit a doctor or a dentist, to exercise, and generally take care of your wellbeing? And how are you going to manage some quality time to spend with your family or pursue your hobbies? Is it any wonder that so many of us find it challenging to be healthy and find time for ourselves amid a rigid work schedule? And if you have obligations and responsibilities outside of work, like taking care of aging parents, how are you going to fit all that into your day?

According to a 2015 report from the Mental Health Commission of Canada (MHCC), "Stress associated with the workplace lowers productivity, increases short- and long-term absences and contributes to mental-health problems."

The report goes on to point out, "If you are in a chronically negative, pressured or chaotic workplace, it is tough for even the most resilient employee to continue to manage stress effectively. It really can reduce productivity. It can have health effects, and

I don't just mean health effects like depression or anxiety, but gastrointestinal problems, autoimmune problems, all sorts of conditions."

So there is no doubt that a workforce, especially a very strict and rigid one, can make employees unhealthy. But if you give them some flexibility and leeway, they'll feel like they have some control over their work life and, subsequently, their personal life as well.

Creating an employee-friendly workplace

If you are an employer, you might be concerned about the huge changes you'd have to make in your organization in order to accommodate the wishes of your workforce. But the good news is that the adjustments don't need to be major; even small modifications can have a significant (and positive!) impact on your employees' welfare.

For instance, one major concern a lot of office workers have is the volume of emails they have to handle in any given day. In fact, a Pew Research Center study found that over 50% of employees check their work email on the weekends and 34% of them check email on vacation.

In my own career, I have had inboxes with well over 1,000 emails that I read once but had no time really to go back to revisit them as the day has passed. I did, of course, action them on the day of, or had to set up flags to go back to some of them so that I would not lose track of what had to be addressed. But I never have any time to go back and clean up my inbox, making sure I didn't miss anything or file away something important.

I know there are a lot of office workers out there who can't keep on top of their emails; reading, sorting according to importance, and responding would require a 24/7 schedule.

So a good place to start implementing a less stressful work environment is to create an email protocol. The first guideline should be the one discouraging the treatment of emails after official business hours. But I would go further. One company for example, forbade any internal emails for a whole week, just to give people the chance to get out of their office, out of their chairs, and go talk to their colleagues, or pick up the phone. It significantly decreased the traffic of emails and increased person-to-person interactions. By the same token, employers can try to reduce the amount of red tape in their organizations. Ensure that employees' time isn't wasted on unnecessary paperwork and procedures.

Some improvements in the workplace happen, literally, by accident. For example, some years ago the CEO of AETNA, which is the third-largest health insurance in the US, had a ski accident that left him disabled for about a year. That prompted him to offer meditation, yoga and acupuncture sessions for all his employees. Afterwards, he hired a university to look at the results of how these measures benefitted AETNA's workplace. The outcome showed a 7% drop in their healthcare costs in one year, as well as additional 62 minutes of productivity per employee per week. This is a good example of how small changes can yield big results.

As already discussed in previous chapters, well-being programs like the one at AETNA could be very beneficial in fostering a healthy and happy workplace, and creating long-lasting employee engagement. But there are other measures as well. For instance:

- Give employees some control / flexibility over how they do their work. But because not all workers know how to structure their time for best performance and productivity, help them develop prioritizing and organizing skills –through a workshop, seminar, or any other way.

- Set realistic goals. Expect the employee to do the work he or she had been hired for. Don't assign tasks that are above their level of competence since this will set them up for failure and, consequently, cause stress and frustration.

- Praise employees for the work well done. It is human nature to criticize rather than compliment. But praise, gratitude, and appreciation should never go unexpressed.

- A study by consultants at Manpower Group found that over 35% of people eat lunch at their desk every day and most employees never take enough breaks to relax and renew their energy. Encourage your employees to have a one-hour lunch and a couple of 15-minute breaks throughout the day.

- If the weather is nice, schedule a "walking meeting" so your subordinates have a chance to get out of the office on a regular basis and enjoy some fresh air.

Three elements of building a worker-friendly corporate culture

Basically, creating workforce engagement comes down to three things: a need for more mutual trust between employees and employers, a need to empower employees, and a need for flexibility.

Let's talk about trust first. As you know, no relationship – be it personal, social, or professional – can be sustained without trust. Yet, there is an inclination among many employers to think that their workers will take advantage if allowed flexibility to manage their own time or make their own work-related decisions. True, there will also be people who will break the bonds of trust but, thankfully, most individuals are honest and responsible – and want to be treated as such.

Experts agree that trust is essential for boosting employee engagement and motivation. According to Harvard Business Review, (HBR) employers can build trust in their organizations by:

- **Making connections** – in other words, getting to know your employees and letting them know you.

- **Being transparent and truthful** – "Share as much as you can about the current health and future goals of the company," HBR suggests. "Otherwise, you'll find yourself constantly battling the rumor mill."

- **Encouraging rather than commanding**. "You don't succeed in the long run by telling people what to do. You have to motivate them to do it," HBR points out, adding that this entails "delegating tasks and granting as much autonomy as possible, while also making it clear what your expectations are and how performance will be measured. People will trust you if you trust them."

- **Admitting mistakes and accepting responsibility**. "Instead of casting blame for layoffs or poor profits, stress that it is the company — and your own leadership — that need to improve. This signals that you don't believe different rules apply to you than to others in the organization," HBR notes.

What about the empowerment? It is closely tied to trust, because to be able to empower your employees – to give them the ability to do the job the way they believe will be optimal - you should be able to trust them. We talk a lot in this book about allowing workers to manage their own time. In companies like Crew Labs, or Mindvalley, where employees are so engaged that the management had to put in place a maximum work week of 45 hours, employees are free to work whenever and wherever it suits them, but they have to cap it at 45.

Compare this approach to other, more traditional companies where there is actually a struggle to have employees work their mandated 35 or 40 hours. Mindvalley is struggling to get its workforce to not exceed 45 hours, which is five hours more than the majority of employers get from their workforce. So the message here is clear: When employees feel empowered to succeed and believe that the goals of the company are aligned with their own, they'll work harder.

Empowerment also means allowing the decisions to be made at the right level. As the upper management is usually considered to be the sole authority in an organization, they unilaterally make all the decisions and leave no room for their subordinates. I have been an executive in various companies where I had absolutely no power of authority. Sure, I could decide on very minor matters, like making an exception for one individual employee. But when it came to making any significant changes in my department, I had to defer to a superior, even though I was hired for my expertise and should have been entrusted to make decisions in my own department. Such an approach, as you can imagine, makes for a very disengaged and disheartened worker.

On the other hand, an empowered employee who feels valued and trusted will be a satisfied, loyal, and productive worker. For example, Toyota hands over responsibilities of identifying and solving production problems to its shop-floor employees. That's because the management knows these workers are better qualified than the CEOs to handle this task.

The result of this worker empowerment can be seen in an anonymous survey Toyota conducts every two years. It shows that employee satisfaction is highest it has ever been - between 69.2% (shop floor) and 73.9% (administrative and engineering).

Let's move on to flexibility, which includes (but is not limited to) part-time work, telecommuting, compressed work week, and job sharing. We discussed this approach before, but it is so very important in the corporate structure that I'd like to touch on it again.

Flexibility is the result of trust and empowerment, in a sense that if the employers trust their workforce to empower it, it also trusts it enough to give it flexibility. So it is really a package deal.

Basically, a flexible approach bends the rules of the traditional workplace, such as fixed hours, locations, and job responsibilities to create a more employee-friendly environment. How and where the work is done is less important than the quality and creativity of the results. This can be achieved when managers surround themselves with – yes, trustworthy and empowered – employees who don't have to be managed. When that happens, numerous benefits follow suit.

I've witnessed this myself. I gave flexibility to small groups of 10 or 12 employees as to how or where they worked, as long as they delivered good results. I trusted each of them to do their job and gave them the authority to make decisions. Of course, sometimes they might have had to inform me about their chosen course of action prior to implementing those measures, especially in more rigid environment where I myself had little authority, but it was still their decision. I was amazed by how well these people performed. They felt energized, loved coming to work, felt that their contribution was impactful, and found satisfaction in their job. I was able to change the ambience very quickly after coming on board just by following my three principles.

Interestingly, when people want to come to work, they don't use their sick leave the same way. They don't take sick days. The best way to handle the need for time away from work is flexibility. "Sick leave," "annual leave," and "vacation" are all very old terms that we've used since the '70s. You want to maybe just have a full-on bucket of days that people can take.

That's another example of something that can be changed. For workplaces where it is felt to be appropriate, you bundle up leave into one category: "You get 20 days, and it's for sick days, vacation, etc." You also allow unpaid leave for when it is needed. I have come across companies where it was nearly impossible to take unpaid time off.

So let's play this out: as much as you want to plan ahead, you could run out of days before the year ends. It has happened to me - my children were sick more often than usual and I had to take my vacation days to stay home, as I did not feel I was really productive on some of those days to legitimately say I was working from home. Having no other alternative but to use vacation days, that is what I took. Well, I ran out of my vacation days by the beginning of December. This meant no time off during the Christmas holiday to spend with my children at home, or with them if they got sick during December. The pressure then was on my spouse to be able to take the time away from his work. This scenario is not unique or exceptional – a lot of people who work in the traditional, rigid environment face the same challenges.

Does this kind of situation make any sense? Does it contribute to a happy work culture, or does create stress and unhealthy workforce? I would have happily taken an unpaid day instead of having the stress of not been able to miss work. The reality is, employers cannot predict absenteeism for the mere fact that they cannot predict illness. That was a premise we had at Canada Post when we put "personal days" in place. Even if an employee called in the same day to say he wouldn't be coming in and not explaining why, it was no different from an employee unable to come to work because of illness. Therefore, employees did not have to give a reason for missing work; they just took a personal day. This kind of corporate culture spells out respect for an employee.

It also takes away the stigma around taking a sick day. How many of us have wondered: "Am I sick enough to take a day off?" "Oh, I'll still go to work because it'll look good." The constant worrying about being judged does not lead to a healthy working environment.

Maybe you really are sick or perhaps you are just stressed out and need a personal day off to relax and get back on track. In a trusting, empowering, and flexible workplace, you don't need to be worried about that. And in this kind of corporate culture, nobody will think that you are slacking off or taking advantage of your employer if you take time off.

The evolution of the workforce must allow room for, and even encourage, the development of personal life. Employees should feel able have a fulfilling life outside of work without being made to feel guilty about it (remember the work-life balance I mentioned in a previous chapter?). So investing in your workers' outside life will be beneficial.

The flip side of the coin is this: If you don't want to trust your employees, empower them, or offer flexible work hours in order to save company money, you just might have to spend *more,* not less, in the end. You'll have higher costs due to increased incidence of medications and disability, absenteeism, low performance and productivity, as well as disenchanted workforce that feels no loyalty to you.

Now, giving employees flexibility doesn't mean they are free to run loose, so to speak. Even in a flexible work environment, there needs to be a structure put in place to ensure that things are running smoothly. If someone is going on vacation, for instance, he or she can't just take off and leave the workload behind. Instead, this employee should make arrangements with a co-worker or manager to keep an eye on the work, or follow up with clients - whatever steps are required. Remember: being flexible doesn't mean being irresponsible!

The best way to ensure such a model works in your organization is to set up guidelines for flexible work, rather than leave it up to individual interpretation. For instance, make sure there is good communication with employees about their obligations and responsibilities. Emphasize to them that even though their work arrangement is flexible, they will still be held accountable for their performance and meeting customer demands; in other words, the results they deliver must justify the trust you've placed in them and the leeway you've given them.

Are you still skeptical about this model? Allow it to happen, before refusing it. If it doesn't work right away, try to see how maybe your old way of thinking is keeping you from making it successful. Change is never easy, but it doesn't mean you shouldn't try.

Points to remember:

A healthy workplace relies on three elements: trust, empowerment, and flexibility. These components are inter-related, each one building on the other.

Most traditional organizations lack this kind of corporate culture, which nurtures and fosters motivation and engagement on the part of the workforce.

In the next, final chapter, I will summarize all the important points made throughout this book.

CHAPTER 9:
Another Look at Key Points

THROUGHOUT THIS BOOK, we covered three topics: 1) The new challenges organizations are facing today; 2) the impact those challenges are having on the bottom line; and 3) what can be done to resolve these problems in an effective and sustainable way.

In these three respects, by the way, Canada is no different from the United States or, for that matter, other developed nations, so problems and solutions are similar across the board.

There is a lot of information provided in this book. In case you haven't retained all of the essential points, it's a good idea to "revisit" them once more.

First, let's review point #1: the challenges a lot of companies are facing in the 21st century and the reasons behind these problems.

Longevity: a double-edged sword

According to data from the World Bank, average life expectancy in Canada right now is 81.2 years. Compare that to 50 years an average Canadian was expected to reach in 1900, and you get an astonishing 62% increase in the lifespan.

You may be wondering why this expanded lifespan is a double-edged sword, especially as it relates to corporate costs.

First of all, this means that for the first time in recorded history, we now have five generations in the labor market.

There are maturists, born between 1924 and 1945; the baby boomers that followed from 1946 to 1964; Generation X up to 1980; Generation Y up to 1995; and the newest Generation Z, born after 1995.

The maturists make up only 3% of the labor force. Approximately 33% are baby boomers, 35% are Generation X, 29% Generation Y, and the millennial or Generation Z are just starting to get into the labor market.

Why is this a problem? Because when workplace pensions started to be introduced in Canada, the retirement age was 65, but the average worker didn't live long enough to collect his benefits. This is to say that traditional plans were not designed to cover multi-generational workforce we have today. So pension plans will cost more money for a longer time.

Employers carry the burden of expensive plans they've put in place for the older generation that should have retired already but is still active on the labor market. (As stated, maturists and boomers constitute about 36% of the workforce).

This leads to the second point: with age, people get sick more often. And when older workers have health issues, especially serious or chronic ones, they will have direct impact on the company's profitability.

We know that the average age for an employee on long-term disability is over 45. The cost of drugs peaks at around 55, so employees 55 and older are the more expensive members of a benefits plan. These people cost money in several ways:

The organization may have insurance to cover disability, but it still costs money. (When your disability premiums increase - and we've seen it happen in the last few years when disability incidence has risen and costs have gone up by 15 to 30% yearly - it is a strain on the employer.)

The premium is likely to be equal to the disability payment that the carrier is paying. So for every person on disability, the employer still pays 60% of his or her salary and gets nothing – in terms of productivity– in return.

But there is more: you will probably have to replace the sick person in your workforce. That would entail paying 100% of his salary, plus whatever you pay the replacement worker.

Add to this mix the additional low interest rates and low returns on investment linked to the slow global economy that affect pension plans in particular, and you can see why so many employers are forced to cut costs.

Strategies and solutions: being pro-active

We know what the problems are and where they originated.

Fortunately, even though things appear to be pretty grim right now, there *are* ways for organizations to save money, while fostering a happy and engaged workforce. It all comes down to creating a healthy work-life balance for your employees.

It may sound difficult, but this does not have to be a complex or long-winded process: often, costs can be reduced immediately by creating an employee-friendly work environment that will boost performance and productivity, all of which will save you money in the long run.

Some of these strategies include offering your employees flexible work (part time, shorter work week, telecommuting, etc.); wellbeing programs, and some control over how they perform their duties.

Studies show that creating employee loyalty strategies like the ones mentioned above could save significant costs – for instance in unscheduled leaves and in workers' compensation claims.

There is no doubt that businesses, which face not only financial problems these days but also the increasingly competitive environment, have to adapt to the new reality – it's no longer an option but a necessity. The most important ingredient of success is a company's ability to create and retain engaged workforce because it will:

- Increase productivity, performance and profitability

- Improve customer relationships

- Stimulate greater creativity

- Build teamwork

- Reduce absenteeism and turnover

In previous chapters, I gave you some examples of forward-thinking companies that have implemented various methods to foster workforce engagement. But there are many more organizations that went the extra mile to create a healthy life-work balance for their employees.

A few years ago, the job search engine Indeed. com identified 25 large U.S. corporations that are leaders in this field. They are a good example of various engagement-boosting strategies many other organizations can implement.

Topping the list, according to Forbes magazine, was Colgate-Palmolive, which employs 35,000 workers. Its management "sets realistic expectations for employees, promotes time management skills and clearly communicates," Forbes' report of the findings notes. In addition, Colgate-Palmolive "offers some great benefits, such as flexible work hours, telecommute options, and nearby back-up childcare centers, which is a nice perk for work-at-home parents. As a result, Colgate-Palmolive has a high rate of employee retention, which is a testament to their culture."

Ranking second was Wegmans, a major regional supermarket chain and one of the largest private companies in the U.S. At this family-owned business, which employs over 44,000 people, "management works to make employees feel independent and valuable," Forbes pointed out. "Wegmans has a reputation for working with part-time employees who are still students to create flexible schedules. The typical workday is fun and energetic, and employees develop great relationships with one another, which supports the overall feeling of family."

Other companies have also made the cut. For instance, Walt Disney was recognized "for their focus on training and team building, as well as the happiness of their employees," while Google is known for "promoting flexible schedules and personal and professional balance, where employees learn how to manage their time, multitask and collaborate."

One thing all the 25 companies have in common is a worker-friendly corporate environment and culture, which provide just the right life-work balance that motivates employees to succeed.

Now, you might be thinking that the Indeed survey focused only on large corporations. But what about small businesses?

A few years ago, Dale Carnegie Training carried out a study to find out how organizations with less than 1,000 people can keep their employees engaged

The survey showed that qualities workers at these companies valued the most were "Being trusted to do my job" and "Being able to do my job with limited oversight."

The survey listed the following "functional attributes" of engaged employees:

- You are given help or support when you need it (67%)

- Senior management is honest with its employees (65%)

- There is good/effective communication at the company (63%)

- You positively impact the quality of your company's products or service (61%)

- You do work that varies and is interesting (52%)

- You have an "open door" policy at your company (48%)

- You have access to training programs for technical and soft skills (48%)

- You have compensation increases above the cost of living (46%)

All this goes to prove that there is a strong connection between employee engagement and an organization's growth and financial success.

The other side of the coin

Let me repeat what I just said before: creating an employee-friendly workplace is no longer an option but a necessity.

However, not all organizations subscribe to this thinking.

According to a recent Gallup poll conducted among 80,844 U.S workers, only 32% considered themselves engaged in their jobs in 2015. As the chart, below, shows that is a 3% increase over 2011, but still a low average.

U.S. Employee Engagement, 2011-2015
Yearly averages

% Engaged employees

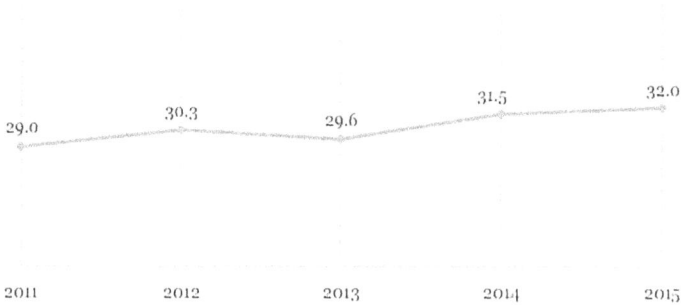

29.0   30.3   29.6   31.5   32.0

2011   2012   2013   2014   2015

GALLUP

According to Gallup, these "disengaged" workers do nothing to boost the company's performance or productivity: they "show up and kill time, doing the minimum required with little extra effort to go out of their way for customers. They are less vigilant, more likely to miss work and change jobs when new opportunities arise. They are thinking about lunch or their next break. Not engaged employees are either 'checked out' or attempting to get their job done with little or no management support."

The above study was done in the United States, but similar research had been carried out in Canada as well. Not surprisingly, its results are, at their core, in line with the U.S. findings (which goes to prove that the issue of employee (dis)engagement transcends borders.

Earlier in 2016, the Conference Board of Canada surveyed 400 Canadian employees and found that only 27% considered themselves to be "highly engaged" in their companies.

In its report, Conference Board identifies "best practices for improving employee engagement, including: leadership training, decentralized accountability, interesting and challenging work and empowerment are good investments for increasing employee engagement."

Why is this stagnating attitude so prevalent and, even more importantly, who is to blame – the unmotivated workers or the employers?

The answer could be that many organizations are not pro-active enough (or at all) in investing in employee engagement.

Here are some of the reasons why companies neglect to create an engaging environment:

Reason #1: Employers misjudge their workforce's commitment

This is akin to burying one's head in the sand: CEOs may be so far removed from their employees that they don't know – or perhaps don't care to know – what the people think of their working conditions, what grievances they may have, and what improvements they would want to see in the workplace. In other words, total lack of communication and interest from the management is to blame.

Reason #2: Bosses don't care about the wellbeing of their employees.

It's a sad reality that some employers don't have their workers' best interests at heart. They don't create a corporate culture where employees feel that they are trusted, appreciated, and rewarded for their efforts. No wonder such an environment is not conducive to employee engagement.

Reason #3: Employers don't understand the importance of creating worker engagement.

Or maybe they do, but they have other priorities on their "to-do" list. (On the positive side, vast majority of employers polled in this year's Workplace America survey ranked employee engagement as their organization's key strategy.)

Reason #4: Organizations don't want to change anything

Very often, the concept of change is not a part of corporate culture. Many employers may be thinking: "We've done things this way for a long time and it's been just fine. If it's not broken, don't fix it."

Reason #5: *They think it's too expensive or just don't know how to go about it*

Employers may not be willing to invest in implementing the system because they think it's not worth the outlay of money. Or perhaps they believe the process is too complicated and are not even willing to try.

Actually, the process of "measuring" employee engagement can be simple or complex – depending on how it is set up. A lot of companies use tools like happiness surveys, feedback, pulse checks, and culture assessments, all of which should solicit the input of all employees at every level of the corporate ladder.

Points to remember:

Organizations are dealing with financial dilemmas brought on by, among other factors, runaway costs of the pension and benefits programs.

Among the most effective strategies and solutions to increase the "3P's — productivity, performance, and profitability — are the ones that emphasize employee engagement.

In the next, final chapter, I will outline my solutions to the pressing problems faced by organizations today: increasing costs of benefits related to rising rates of illness and disability, as well as strategies for a better and healthier workplace.

CONCLUSION

Helping You Create a Better and Sounder Organization

NOW THAT WE'VE examined various problems arising – either directly or indirectly – from the pension and benefits crisis, the question is: where do we go from here? At the end of the day, that is the one thing every organization is (or at least should be) looking into.

The problems are serious, yes, but solutions are there. I have given you some ideas as to what can be done to create a positive workplace with productive and engaged employees, all the while cutting costs and boosting your bottom line. My goal here has been to show the current state of things in a different light – by bringing you real and specific examples any employer can implement. Let's look again at my 5-point plan for your organization:

1. *Take a look at reality in your organization*

Does your company experience the problems I have outlined in this book?

- Escalating disability and drug costs;

- Little or no salary increase in years;

- Multiple generations with different needs based on where they are in the life cycle;

- Low engagement; the need for change to enhance the employee experience and secure engagement.

If you do see any (or all) of these signs in your organization, let me help you with a quick assessment of your situation. If you have consultants helping you manage your pension and benefits plan, my role would be complementary to theirs. I will not redo any of the analysis, but would look at the information you have to provide a diagnostic of what you need to do to redirect your company towards the goal at hand. I can suggest some quick changes that will help the organization.

2. *The major shift needed in our way of finding solutions*

This step means that there is a need for real change in addressing the problem. Cost containment and reducing benefits is not the optimal solution to the current situation. This will just create other problems, like lack of coverage for employees, loss of engagement and trust in the company. I can help you refocus your efforts on the <u>right</u> solutions: addressing the workplace problems causing a lot of the costs that you are incurring.

3. Create solutions that deliver on promises and adapt to changes

The focus will be on finding the right way in your organization to create a relationship of trust between employer and employee - the kind of relationship that fosters flexibility and empowerment, so that employees can thrive. I chose to work for Great-West Life because of their investment in the workplace, by developing a community support with the website www.workplacestrategiesformentalhealth.com. This site offers a variety of free tools available to everyone - credible, evidence-based tools and resources to help with the prevention, support, and management of employees' mental health issues. As it can be difficult to allocate resources to get this done, I can assist you in integrating solutions that will create real change that will address the core problem. I will help you find the best options for your organization and make them an integral part of your culture, so that your company can evolve, as it needs to, adapting to today's reality.

4. Create leadership and engagement based on the needs of the workforce

The solutions found in point # 3 will include education for your leadership that will help create the right changes in your organization. Whether the need is to assist in change or performance management, workplace stressors, leadership style, etc., I can help you make the right choices and achieve positive results.

5. *Capitalize on the strengths of happy employees from every generation to create a thriving organization*

Actually, that's the main message of this book: how to avoid escalation of costs to the point where they will no longer be affordable, preventing you from being able to buy the insurance you need; in the worst-case scenario, you might even have to close your organization.

That is why it is so important – crucial, actually – to tap into the strengths and abilities of employees from every generation. Creating a thriving organization does take work, courage, and enlightened mindset but, as explained in this book, it will bring tremendous rewards.

When your employees come to work with the feeling of inclusion, of being part of something, they will enjoy working with you (as oppose to for you). Naturally things will improve.

And the solution can be reached at an affordable cost. I can consult with you for a complimentary 90-minute audit of your organization and your specific plans. From there, I can give you my assessment of what you need done. I can then assist you further to achieve the newly found goals. I can be reached at renee.couture@ucconsulting.ca or by phone at 613-301-5550.

www.ingramcontent.com/pod-product-compliance
Lightning Source LLC
Chambersburg PA
CBHW062010200326

41519CB00017B/4742